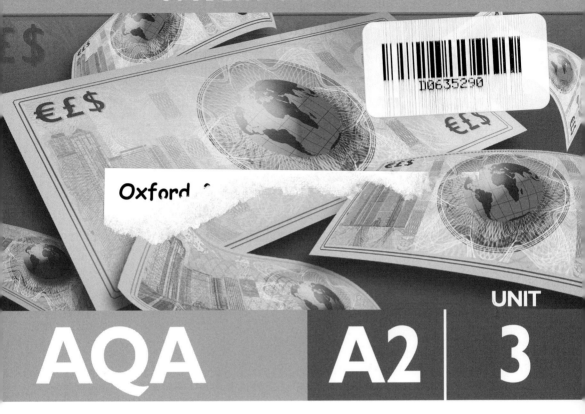

AQA

A2

3

Economics

Business Economics and the Distribution of Income

Ray Powell

Philip Allan Updates, an imprint of Hodder Education, an Hachette UK company, Market Place, Deddington, Oxfordshire, OX15 0SE

Orders

Bookpoint Ltd, 130 Milton Park, Abingdon, Oxfordshire, OX14 4SB

tel: 01235 827720

fax: 01235 400454

e-mail: uk.orders@bookpoint.co.uk

Lines are open 9.00 a.m.–5.00 p.m., Monday to Saturday, with a 24-hour message answering service. You can also order through the Philip Allan Updates website: www.philipallan.co.uk

ISBN 978-0-340-94747-0

First printed 2009
Impression number 5 4 3
Year 2013 2012 2011 2010

This Guide has been written specifically to support students preparing for the AQA A2 Economics Unit 3 examination. The content has been neither approved nor endorsed by AQA and remains the sole responsibility of the author.

Typeset by Phoenix Photosetting, Chatham, Kent
Printed by MPG Books, Bodmin

Hachette UK's policy is to use papers that are natural, renewable and recyclable products and made from wood grown in sustainable forests. The logging and manufacturing processes are expected to conform to the environmental regulations of the country of origin.

P1651

Contents

Introduction

Examinable skills 4

Data-response skills 4

Essay question skills 7

The synoptic requirement of the Unit 3 examination 7

Checklist of relevant Unit 1 terms 8

Stretch and challenge and achieving the A* grade 8

Revision planning 10

■ ■ ■

Content Guidance

About this section 14

Introduction to the specification 15

Firms, production and costs 17

Market structure and sales revenue 22

Perfect competition and monopoly 27

Oligopoly 31

Evaluating market structures 36

Industrial policy 42

Market failure, government failure and cost–benefit analysis 47

The labour market 52

Income, wealth and poverty 59

■ ■ ■

Questions and Answers

About this section 68

Data-response questions

The global context

Q1 The global oil market and UK firms 69

Q2 The effect of the collapse of General Motors on the UK car industry 75

Q3 Global competition and the UK call centre industry 82

The European Union context

Q4 The Single European Market and UK sports markets 87

Q5 Overfishing and the EU's Common Fisheries Policy 92

Q6 EU labour migration and the UK 96

Essay questions

Q1 Perfect competition, monopoly and the water industry 101

Q2 Price-setting for a rock concert 105

Q3 The causes of poverty and government policies to reduce poverty 109

Introduction

The aim of this guide is to prepare students for the AQA Advanced Level examination assessing A2 Unit 3: Business Economics and the Distribution of Income. You should use the guide as follows:

(1) Read the introduction.

(2) The second and third sections of the book should then be used as supplements to other resources, such as class notes, textbooks, *Economic Review* magazine and *AS/A-Level Economics Revision Notes*. (The last two of these are published by Philip Allan Updates.) Because it contains summaries rather than in-depth coverage of all the topics in the specification, you should not use the guide as your sole learning resource during the main part of the course. However, you may well decide to use the guide as the main resource in your revision programme. You are strongly advised to make full use of the Questions and Answers section, especially in the revision period when you should be concentrating on improving your examination skills.

Examinable skills

The Unit examination is 2 hours long, has a maximum mark of 80 and contains two sections, Section A and Section B, which each count for 40 marks. There are two data-response questions (DRQs) in Section A, of which you should answer one. Question 1 is set on the **global context** and Question 2 is set on the **European Union context**. There are *three* essay questions (EQs) in Section B, of which you should answer *one*. There are no multiple-choice questions in either of the A2 Unit examination papers.

The examination has four assessment objectives (AOs): knowledge; application; analysis and evaluation, for which the requirements to achieve a grade A are set out in Table 1 on p. 5.

In the A2 examination, 52% of the marks are awarded for lower-level skills and 48% for higher-level skills (with analysis and evaluation each accounting for 24%). This means the A2 Unit examinations are more difficult than the AS Unit exams, where only 40% of the total marks are awarded for the higher-level skills.

Data-response skills

Both the data-response questions in Section A of the Unit 3 exam paper contain three sub-questions. The mark allocation from May 2010 will be as follows: first sub-question 5 marks; second sub-question 10 marks; third sub-question 25 marks, which add to the total of 40 marks for the whole question.

Table 1 The four examination assessment objectives

	Assessment objective 1	Assessment objective 2	Assessment objective 3	Assessment objective 4
Assessment objectives	Demonstrate knowledge and understanding of the specified content	Apply knowledge and understanding of the specified content to problems and issues arising from both familiar and unfamiliar situations	Analyse economic problems and issues	Evaluate economic arguments and evidence, making informed judgements
A/B boundary performance descriptions	Candidates characteristically demonstrate across the AS and A2 specifications: a) detailed knowledge of a range of facts and concepts b) clear understanding of: ● terminology ● institutions ● models c) detailed knowledge and clear understanding of the inter-connections between the different elements of the subject content	Candidates characteristically apply clearly and effectively: ● concepts ● numerical and graphical techniques ● theories and models ● terminology to complex issues arising in familiar and unfamiliar situations	Candidates characteristically: a) select relevant concepts, models, theories and techniques b) demonstrate, for the most part, development of logical explanations for complex economic problems and issues, with focus and relevance	Candidates characteristically evaluate effectively complex economic arguments: ● prioritise evidence and arguments ● make reasoned judgements ● reach and present supported conclusions ● make reasoned recommendations

The Unit 3 data-response questions contain slightly more data than AS data-response questions in the Unit 1 and 2 examinations. The layout and structure of the question will be similar to the six data-response questions in the Questions and Answers section of this guide. Each question is likely to contain two or three sets of data. With three data sets, the data will be labelled Extract A, Extract B and Extract C (for Question 1) and Extract D, Extract E and Extract F (for Question 2). One set of data is likely to be numerical, for example a line graph, a bar graph, a pie graph or a table. The other data set(s) will be text.

An incline of difficulty will be built into each DRQ, with the earlier parts of the question being the most straightforward. Typically, the key instruction words for each part of the DRQ will be:

(1) Compare (or possibly **identify**)

(2) Explain (or possibly **analyse**, or explain a term or concept, followed by analyse an issue)

(3) Evaluate (or possibly **assess** or **do you agree?**, together with **justify your argument**)

The first two parts of the questions will be marked using an **issue-based mark scheme** which lists the marks that can be awarded for the particular issues (and associated development) that might be included in the answer. Only lower-level skills (meeting AOs 1 and 2) are tested in part (1) of the questions. The higher-level skill of analysis is tested in parts (2) and (3) of the questions, but evaluation is only tested in part (3), where it accounts for 10 of the available 25 marks.

The final part of each DRQ differs from the earlier parts in three significant ways. First, and most obviously, it carries many more marks — 62.5% of the total marks for the question and 31.25% of the total marks for the whole paper. If you time the examination incorrectly and fail to develop your answer to part (3) beyond a cursory footnote, you will reduce considerably your chance of achieving a grade A, let alone an A*. Second, whereas parts (1) and (2) should be answered quite briefly, you are expected to write an extended answer of least two pages for part (3). Think of this as a full-blown but nevertheless concise essay. Third, as I have already indicated, higher-level skills of **analysis** and particularly **evaluation** are expected in your final answer.

A levels of response mark scheme containing five levels is used for part (3) of each DRQ and for part (2) of all the essay questions in Section B. (Numbered sub-questions are also being used in the essay questions, replacing parts (a) and (b)). You must familiarise yourself with the 'levels' mark scheme and bear it in mind when you practise the last part of data-response questions and essay questions. The key command word, e.g. to evaluate or assess, must be obeyed for your answer to reach the higher Level 4 and Level 5 standards of attainment set out in the levels of response mark scheme. Take special note of the summaries of each level and the number of marks available for each level. These are:

Level 1 A very weak answer (0 to 6 marks)

Level 2 A poor answer but some understanding is shown (7 to 11 marks)

Level 3 An adequate answer with some correct analysis but very limited evaluation (12 to 16 marks)

Level 4 Good analysis but limited evaluation (17 to 21 marks)

Level 5 Good analysis and evaluation (22 to 25 marks)

Your answer must evaluate the different arguments you set out, preferably as you make each argument. With many questions, discussion should centre on evaluating the advantages and disadvantages of a course of action mentioned in the question.

Whether or not you have evaluated each argument as you make it, always try to finish your answer with a conclusion, the nature of which should vary according to the type of discussion or evaluation required. The conclusion might judge the relative strengths of the arguments discussed, possibly highlighting the most important argument. With many questions it is more appropriate to conclude whether, on balance, the case for is stronger than the case against and to provide some credible and reasoned justification for your opinion.

Essay question skills

You must select *one* essay question from a choice of three when answering Section B of the paper. The choice of question is obviously very important. Because business economics accounts for approximately half the specification content, you should expect at least one essay question on the theory of the firm or a related topic. Topics include: the market structures of perfect competition and monopoly, production and cost theory, how and why firms grow, and aspects of the government's industrial policy such as competition policy, regulation and deregulation.

You should also expect one essay question on the labour market, and/or distributions of income and/or wealth and/or poverty, and one question on another area of the specification, such as market failure and/or government failure, cost–benefit analysis, etc.

The key instruction words for the two parts of each essay question are likely to be:

Explain

Evaluate (or possibly **assess** or **do you agree?**, together with **justify your argument**)

As is the case with the first parts of the data-response question, the first part of the essay question tests the lower-level skills and assessment objectives of knowledge and application. The advice I have already given on how to answer the last part of the data-response questions is equally applicable to answering the second part of your chosen essay question.

The synoptic requirement of the Unit 3 examination

It is important to realise that the Unit 3 and Unit 4 examinations at A-level are **synoptic**. To understand what this means, you should compare the Unit 3 examination with the Unit 1 AS examination on Markets and Market Failure. Questions in the Unit 1 examination must only test knowledge and understanding of terms and concepts set out in the AQA Unit 1 specification. For example, a Unit 1 examination cannot contain a question on a market which requires the candidate to apply a macroeconomic concept (for example, the influence of the economic cycle) to explain a shift of the demand curve in the market. Booms and recessions are in the Unit 2 National Economy specification and not in the Unit 1 specification.

A question such as this could, however, appear in the Unit 3 examination. It illustrates both vertical synopticity and horizontal synopticity. **Horizontal synopticity** requires the application of a Unit 4 macroeconomic concept or theory to answer a Unit 3 microeconomic question. By contrast, **vertical synopticity** requires the use of AS microeconomic concepts and theories (in the Unit 1 specification) to answer Unit 3 microeconomic questions. It is important to note the following points.

(1) There is no mention of supply and demand (except in the context of the labour market) in the Unit 3 specification, yet it is vital that you remember and revise this extremely important element of microeconomics, including elasticity.

(2) Although public goods and externalities are mentioned in the Unit 3 specification, other market failures such as merit and demerit goods are not mentioned. However, you may be required in the Unit 3 examination to develop and extend material learnt for AS, particularly in relation to resource allocation and misallocation. You must learn also how to apply the key A2 concept of allocative efficiency.

Checklist of relevant Unit 1 terms

Here is a checklist of Unit 1 AS terms, concepts and theories, not mentioned in the Unit 3 specification, which might be needed for the Unit 3 exam:
- the purpose of economic activity
- the economic problem, scarcity, the need for choice and opportunity cost
- economic resources and factors of production
- the nature of a competitive market
- supply and demand diagrams, equilibrium, disequilibrium, excess demand, excess supply
- shifts of demand and supply curves
- elasticity: price elasticity of demand and supply, income elasticity of demand, cross elasticity of demand
- substitutes, complementary goods and derived demand
- normal goods and inferior goods
- how changes in one market can affect other markets
- the signalling, incentive and rationing (allocative) functions of prices
- cost curve diagrams, economies and diseconomies of scale
- causes of market failure: public goods, positive and negative externalities, merit goods, demerit goods, together with relevant marginal private, external and social cost and benefit diagrams, monopoly and income inequalities as market failures
- government policies to make markets work better and to correct market failure: taxation, subsidy, redistribution, regulation, tradable permits to pollute, price controls, buffer stock policies
- government failure

Stretch and challenge and achieving the A* grade

The questions set in Unit 3 and Unit 4 examinations offer you the opportunity of being 'stretched and challenged' in your responses to the questions you choose to answer.

Stretch and challenge is designed to allow the brightest students the opportunity to demonstrate the full extent of their knowledge and skills.

According to AQA, the requirement to set questions in the Unit 3 and Unit 4 exams that stretch and challenge exam candidates is met by the parts of each of the data-response and essay questions that call for extended writing in the answers. These are the final parts of both the data-response questions and the essay questions. The higher skill levels (Levels 4 and 5) of the Levels Mark Scheme indicate the high expectations which candidates are required to meet in order to achieve high marks. The requirement for the questions set in the new A2 examination papers to stretch and challenge will be met by ensuring that mark schemes give due reward to candidates displaying the higher-level skills of analysis and evaluation in their answers to the last part of their chosen questions.

Achieving an A* grade

Stretch and challenge questions provide the opportunity to achieve an A* grade overall at A-level. Like the A* grade at GCSE, the A-level A* grade attempts to address the need for greater differentiation between the most able and the slightly less able students. The most able students should gain an A* grade, while the slightly less able should achieve the standard A grade. Most importantly, a very good performance at A2 is needed for an A* grade to be earned. A high mark at AS, accompanied by reasonable but not excellent performance at A2, may achieve an A grade, but not an A* in the overall A-level award that results from adding up the candidate's AS and A2 marks.

For A2 and the overall A-level, the **Uniform Mark Scale (UMS)** needed to gain an A grade and an A* grade are shown below. (The examiner who marks the exam paper awards a **'raw' mark**, which is then converted into a UMS mark, for which the possible total mark per Unit exam is 100, with 80 being the grade boundary for grade A.)

Table 2 Uniform Mark Scale (UMS) requirements for grades A and A*

AS		A2	
	Maximum mark		Maximum mark
Unit 1	100	Unit 3	100
Unit 2	100	Unit 4	100
Total	200	Total	200
Grade A boundary	160	Grade A boundary	160
	A-level (AS and A2)		
Total	400		
Grade A boundary	320		
A* requirement	320 overall, with 180 achieved at A2		

Revision planning

The revision strategy below is based on the use of this guide, supplemented by other resources such as the notes you have built up over your course of study and favoured textbooks. The programme is designed for the 3-week period before the examination. The strategy assumes you are revising at least two other A-level subjects (and for the Unit 4: National and International Economy examination) during the same period, but are able to devote a session of 2 hours (plus half an hour for short breaks) to Unit 3 every other day, with shorter follow-up sessions on the intervening days. You should revise solidly for 6 days a week, but allow yourself one day off a week to recharge your batteries. The strategy can be modified to meet your personal needs and preferences: for example, by shortening each revision session and/or extending the sessions over a revision period longer than 3 weeks.

(1) Revise one topic from the Content Guidance section of this guide per revision session. Divide the revision session into four half-hour periods during which you are working solidly and without distraction, interspersed with 10-minute breaks.

(2) Proceed through the topics in the order they appear in the guide:
> Week 1: Topics 1–3
> Week 2: Topics 4–6
> Week 3: Topics 7–9

(3) Vary the activities you undertake in each 30-minute period of a revision session. For example, spend the first 30 minutes reading through the 'Essential information' section of the topic. List key terms and concepts on a piece of paper. After a short break, use the second 30-minute period to check more fully the meaning of the key terms and concepts in your class notes and/or an economics textbook. Then after a second short break, check which essay questions and parts of data-response questions in the Questions and Answers section of the guide test aspects of the topic you are revising. Spend the rest of the 30 minutes answering some or all of the questions. In the final 30-minute period — or perhaps in a follow-up session a day or two later — carefully read through any candidate answers that relate to the parts of the essay question or DRQ covered by the topic, and also read the examiner's comments on the question(s).

To vary your revision programme, and to make sure you reinforce and retain the vital information revised in the longer sessions, you should fit some of the activities suggested below into follow-up sessions. Activities suitable for follow-up and 10-minute sessions include the following:

- Write definitions of some key terms and concepts relating to the topic revised on the previous day. Check each of your definitions against the correct definition in this guide, or in a textbook or your class notes.
- Draw key diagrams relating to the topic. Check any diagram you draw against a correct version of the diagram, making absolutely sure that the diagram is correctly and clearly labelled.

- Whenever you make mistakes, repeat these exercises every day or so, until you have eliminated all the mistakes.
- Answer questions from past AQA examination papers and from AQA's 'Specimen Units and Mark Schemes' booklet, which your teacher should have. Make sure your teacher obtains all the relevant June and January AQA past exam papers that are available at the time you take the examination. Identify and then answer questions from past papers, which relate to the topic just revised. Then spend another follow-up session checking your answer(s) against the AQA mark scheme(s) to see how you could improve your answer(s).

Note: AQA now provides all its resources, including the specification, past exam papers and mark schemes on its website: **www.aqa.org.uk**.

In addition, provided they are registered with e-AQA, your teachers can also access exam papers, mark schemes and examination reports rather earlier, after the exams have finished. Any further information about AQA economics can be obtained from the Economics subject officer, AQA, Stag Hill House, Guildford, GU2 7XJ.

Content
Guidance

In contrast to AS Unit 1: Markets and Market Failure, which is concerned with *elementary* microeconomics, Unit 3: Business Economics and the Distribution of Income centres for the most part on more *advanced* microeconomics. As the specification states, Unit 3 builds on the knowledge and skills developed in Unit 1. It will require you to use and evaluate more complex microeconomic models; for example, perfect competition, monopoly and oligopoly, and to develop further your critical approach to such economic models and methods of enquiry. You will need to demonstrate a realistic understanding of the decisions made by firms and how their behaviour can be affected by the structure and characteristics of the industry. In this Unit, you are required to develop a more formal understanding of economic efficiency and the arguments for and against government intervention in markets than was required at AS level.

The Unit also requires that you understand the operations of the labour market and the factors which influence relative wage rates, poverty and the distribution of income and wealth. You must appreciate the ways in which developments in United Kingdom markets and government microeconomic policy can be related to the global and European Union (EU) contexts.

Examples of issues which could be examined in the **global context** are the impact of globalisation on markets and firms within the UK economy, for example through the increased economic power of multinational (transnational) companies and through a greater international mobility of capital and labour. Environmental issues should also be seen from a global perspective.

Examples of issues in the **EU context** are: increased competitiveness of UK markets resulting from firms' access to the wider EU market, and the potential exposure of UK firms to EU competition policy as well as to UK national competition policy. You should also consider the impact on UK product and labour markets of EU common economic policies (e.g. the Common Agricultural Policy), and of the free movement of labour within the EU.

Unlike in Unit 1, the labour market is an important part of Unit 3. The Unit also includes a number of topics that are linked to the macroeconomic content of Unit 4: The National and International Economy. These are: the distribution of income and wealth, the causes of poverty, and the use of fiscal policy instruments of (taxation and public spending) to reduce poverty and income inequalities.

Introduction to the specification

The AQA specification for Unit 3 contains the following sections.

3.3.1 The firm: objectives, costs and revenues

This specification section covers knowledge of **short-run** and **long-run production** (including the **law of diminishing returns** and **returns to scale**), knowledge of how **cost curves** are derived from production theory in both the short run and the long run, and an understanding of **economies of scale**, **diseconomies of scale** and **minimum efficient scale** in relation to a firm's long-run average cost curve. The concepts of fixed cost and variable cost, and marginal cost, short-run average cost and total cost must also be understood, along with total, average and marginal revenue. You may be required to draw **cost curves** and **revenue curves** from data supplied in the exam question. The concept of the **margin** is particularly important in the Unit 3 specification. Having refreshed your knowledge of marginal private, external and social cost and benefit learnt at AS, at A2 you must also understand the concepts of marginal returns (marginal product), marginal cost and marginal revenue. Knowledge of **profit**, which is the difference between revenue and cost, is required. Although not mentioned in the specification, the concepts of normal and supernormal (or abnormal or above normal) profit are important. You must understand the **profit-maximising objective** of firms, and its relationship to the traditional **theory of the firm**, together with alternative objectives to profit maximisation such as **satisficing**. You must also understand the reason for the separation or **divorce of ownership from control** in modern industrial economies and how this affects the conduct and performance of firms. You must understand how **technological change** and **technical progress** affect the structure of markets and the production and consumption of goods and services, together with the impact of invention, innovation and technological change upon a firm's methods of production, its efficiency and its cost structure.

3.3.2 Competitive markets

This section of the Unit 3 specification introduces the economist's model of **perfect competition**. You must know how, subject to certain assumptions about the absence of externalities and economies of scale, perfect competition results in **efficient resource allocation**. Given these assumptions, consumers benefit from competitive markets. You must be able to handle a formal diagrammatic analysis of perfect competition, in the **short run** and the **long run**, and at the level of both the **whole market** and a **single firm** within the market. Knowledge of methods of competition other than price competition is expected, though such knowledge is likely to be more relevant to an understanding of concentrated markets.

3.3.3 Concentrated markets

This section of the specification covers two important market structures in the real economy: **monopoly** and **oligopoly**, where firms are price-makers rather than price-takers. You must understand **how** and **why firms grow** and the difference between internal growth (organic growth) and external growth via takeover or merger. You must know how to evaluate and compare the conduct and performance of firms within these market structures with the conduct and performance of perfectly competitive firms. You must understand the sources of monopoly power. You may be asked to apply **efficiency concepts** to analyse and evaluate the performance and desirable and less desirable characteristics of monopoly, oligopoly and perfect competition. You must also analyse market structures in terms of gains, losses and transfers of **economic welfare** in the form of **consumer surplus** and **producer surplus**. You must understand how uncertainty and interdependence, in both **competitive oligopoly** and **collusive oligopoly** (for example, in cartels), affect firms' behaviour, leading to different forms of **price setting**, including **price discrimination**. The role of **entry barriers** in protecting monopoly power is also important. You must appreciate how **market contestability** affects industry performance and the roles of sunk costs and hit-and-run competition.

3.3.4 The labour market

This section of the specification requires application of **supply and demand theory** to the economy's labour markets. You must understand how the demand for labour is a derived demand, explained in part by **marginal productivity theory** and the **law of diminishing returns** (in specification section 3.3.1). It is important to distinguish between demand for, and supply of, labour in the *whole* of a labour market, and at the level of a *particular firm* and an *individual worker* within the labour market.

In **perfectly competitive labour markets**, individual firms and workers are passive price-takers at the ruling market wage set in the market as a whole. By contrast, in **monopsony** labour markets, a single employer or buyer of labour has the market power to set the wage rate below the value of the marginal product of labour. Monopsony employers can also engage in wage discrimination, and discrimination according to gender, race or religion. You must understand the various factors that affect the ability of trade unions to influence wages, and analyse the effect on employment of a union setting a wage above the free-market wage, both in a perfectly competitive labour market and in monopsony. You should be able to adapt this knowledge to analyse the effect of a **national minimum wage**. Knowledge of the **distribution of income and wealth** in the UK is expected, and of the factors influencing the distribution.

3.3.5 Government intervention in the market

The specification requires application of efficiency and welfare criteria, particularly **allocative efficiency and inefficiency**, to explain and analyse market failures and related policy solutions. The use of **marginalist analysis** is expected, particularly the use of diagrams learnt at AS, showing marginal private cost and benefit and marginal social cost and benefit. Market failures associated with **environmental change** are likely to figure in examination questions. Explanation, analysis and evaluation of government policies to correct market failure is expected. This may centre on policies such as **taxation** and **regulation**, together with establishing markets in **permits to pollute** and in **property rights**. You must appreciate how government intervention to correct or reduce market failure may create new problems of **government failure** such as regulatory capture, which occurs when regulators, who are meant to protect the interests of consumers, side instead with the producers they are supposed to regulate. When assessing the costs and benefits of government intervention, you must understand the principles of **cost–benefit analysis (CBA)** and be able to evaluate the advantages and disadvantages of using CBA. A number of topics relating to the government's **industrial policy** are important. These are competition policy, public ownership, privatisation, regulation and deregulation of markets, together with some knowledge of competitive tendering, internal markets and public–private partnerships. You must understand the nature of **poverty** and be able to analyse government policies to reduce poverty which aim to make the distribution of income and wealth more equal. When evaluating the success of these policies, you must understand the difference between **absolute poverty** and **relative poverty**, and the difference between **vertical and horizontal equity**.

Firms, production and costs

These notes, which relate to AQA specification sections 3.3.1, prepare you to answer AQA examination questions on:

- firms and their objectives
- production theory
- costs of production

Essential information

Firms and their objectives

There are many different types of business or firm, ranging from very small one-person businesses, performing functions such as painting and decorating, to massive companies such as British Petroleum (BP), at the opposite end of the size spectrum. The latter are often **multinational firms** owning and controlling subsidiary companies and establishments throughout the world. In most instances, the largest companies are also **multi-product firms**, producing and selling different goods and services in a number of different markets.

Economists usually assume that firms have a single business objective — to **maximise profit**. However, real-world firms may have other objectives: to maximise sales revenue; to maximise the growth of the business; or to maximise managerial objectives. The last is significant when there is a divorce of ownership from control in a business, which occurs in large firms organised as public limited companies (plcs). Plcs are owned by thousands of shareholders who employ managers or executives to run the business. As business scandals in the early twenty-first century in firms such as Enron and Worldcom have shown, the managers may pursue their own agendas, maximising their own pay and making decisions that are not in the interest of the owners of the business.

So far I have assumed that firms have a maximising objective, be it profit, sales revenue, growth, or management pay and creature comforts. However, some firms may be best modelled as *satisficers* rather than *maximisers*. Under this assumption, decision makers in firms, be they the owners of small corner shops or the chief executives of huge plcs, may be content with a satisfactory outcome, say satisfactory profit, rather than the best possible outcome. They may be happy with an easy life.

Production

Firms produce goods or services for sale at a price in markets. Production converts inputs into outputs of useful goods and services. The inputs necessary for production to take place, which include the services of **labour**, **capital** and **land**, are known as the **factors of production**. Economists also identify a fourth factor of production, **enterprise** or the entrepreneurial input. The **entrepreneur** is the financial risk taker and decision maker. In a small business, the owner combines both these functions, bearing the financial risks, but also reaping the financial rewards, and deciding such questions as what, how and how much to produce. However, with the divorce between ownership and control in many large firms, the entrepreneurial function is split between owners (shareholders) and the salaried managers they employ.

The short run and the long run

In microeconomic theory, the short run is the period of time in which at least one factor of production is fixed. In the short run, a firm can increase output or supply only by adding more of a variable factor, such as labour, to the fixed factors of production such as capital and land. Also, firms cannot enter or leave a market in the short run. In the long run, all the factors of production are variable and a firm can increase output or supply by changing the *scale* of the factors held fixed in the short run. Only in the long run can a firm either expand the scale of its operations by increasing capacity, or reduce its activities by closing down a plant. The long run is also the time period in which new firms can enter a market or industry and existing firms can leave, providing no barriers exist to prevent freedom of entry and exit.

Short-run production and the law of diminishing returns

Suppose a small manufacturing firm decides to employ only one worker. The worker must be a jack-of-all-trades, doing all tasks involved in production. But if more workers are hired, output can rise at a faster rate than the number of workers employed. This is because the workers benefit from **specialisation** and the **division of labour**, as production tasks are divided between the workers. In this situation, the **marginal product** of labour will increase. Marginal product (marginal returns) is the increase in output that results from adding an extra worker to the labour force.

However, eventually, as more and more workers are combined with the firm's fixed capital, the benefits of further specialisation and division of labour come to an end. The **law of diminishing returns** (also known as the law of diminishing marginal productivity) sets in when the marginal product of labour starts to fall. That is, when one more worker adds less to total output than the previous worker who joined the labour force.

Long-run production and returns to scale

The law of diminishing returns is a short-run law which does not operate in the long run, when a firm can increase the scale of all its inputs or factors of production. You must not confuse the short-run law of diminishing returns with returns to scale which occur only in the long run. With returns to scale there are three possibilities:

- **Increasing returns to scale**. An increase in the scale of all the factors of production causes a more than proportionate increase in output.
- **Decreasing returns to scale**. An increase in the scale of all the factors of production causes a less than proportionate increase in output.
- **Constant returns to scale**. An increase in the scale of all the factors of production causes an exactly proportionate increase in output.

Short-run costs

In the short run, a firm's total costs of production divide into **fixed costs** (the cost of employing the fixed factors of production, such as capital) and **variable costs** (the cost of employing the variable factors of production, such as labour). **Total fixed costs (TFC)**, (overheads), are shown by the constant or horizontal line in the left-hand panel of Figure 1. The right-hand panel shows **average fixed costs (AFC)**, which fall as overheads are spread over larger levels of output.

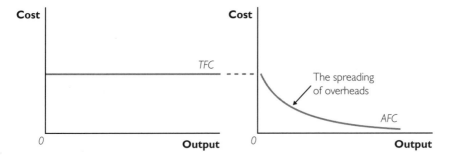

Figure 1 Total fixed costs and average fixed costs

Figure 2 shows an **average variable cost (AVC)** curve, with a **marginal cost (MC)** curve rising and cutting through the lowest point on the *AVC* curve. Marginal cost is the extra cost of producing one more unit of output. The shape of the *MC* curve is explained by marginal productivity theory. As long as the marginal productivity of labour is increasing, then, assuming all workers are paid the same wage rate, the cost of producing an extra unit of output falls. Hence marginal costs fall at low levels of output. But as soon as the law of diminishing returns sets in, each worker hired adds less to total output than the previous worker taken on. Total costs of production rise faster than output, leading to rising marginal costs.

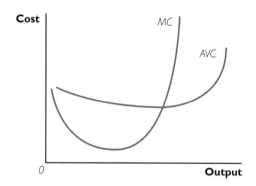

Figure 2 Average variable costs (AVC) and marginal costs (MC)

Figure 2 provides an illustration of the important relationship between any marginal curve and the average curve plotted from the same data:
- when the marginal > the average, the average rises
- when the marginal < the average, the average falls
- when the marginal = the average, the average is constant, neither rising nor falling

The relationship between marginal and average curves has several economic applications: marginal and average product curves (in production theory); marginal and average cost curves (illustrated in Figures 2 and 3); and, as I shall explain in the next topic, marginal and average revenue curves. You must understand this relationship. It does not state that an average curve will rise when the related marginal curve is rising, or that the average curve must fall when the related marginal curve falls. Study Figure 2 carefully. After diminishing returns set in, the *MC* curve starts to rise, but the *AVC* curve continues to fall as long as marginal costs are below average variable costs. Eventually, however, the *MC* curve rises through the *AVC* curve, causing the *AVC* curve also to rise. As a result, the *AVC* curve is U-shaped, with the *MC* curve cutting through the curve at its lowest point.

The left-hand panel of Figure 3 shows how the firm's **average total cost (ATC)** curve is arrived at by adding up the *AFC* and *AVC* curves. The right-hand panel of

Figure 3 shows the *ATC* curve without its two 'building blocks' (*AFC* and *AVC*). The *ATC* curve is U-shaped, showing that average total costs per unit of output first fall and later rise as output is increased. *ATC* must eventually rise because, at high levels of output, any further spreading of fixed costs is insufficient to offset the impact of diminishing returns upon variable costs of production. Eventually, rising marginal costs (which, as I have explained, result from diminishing marginal returns) must cut through and pull up the *ATC* curve.

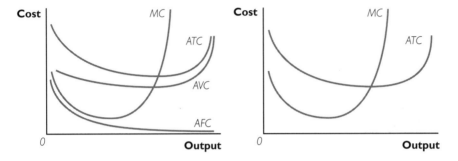

Figure 3 The average total cost curve results from adding **AVC** *to* **AFC**

Long-run average costs, and economies and diseconomies of scale

Just as the short-run law of diminishing returns explains rising marginal costs and (eventually, when marginal costs cut through average total costs) rising average total costs, so I shall now use long-run production theory concepts to explain the firm's long-run average cost (*LRAC*) curve, illustrated in Figure 4. If, as the firm increases the size or scale of all its factors of production, it benefits from increasing returns to scale, the *LRAC* curve falls. Falling long-run average costs are known as **economies of scale**. Conversely, rising long-run average costs are known as **diseconomies of scale**. You should notice that a number of short-run average total cost (*SRATC*) curves, labelled $SRATC_1$, $SRATC_2$ and $SRATC_3$, have been drawn in Figure 4, and that the *LRAC* curve touches (or is tangential to) each *SRATC* curve. Each *SRATC* curve represents a particular short-run size of firm.

The left-hand panel of Figure 4 shows a U-shaped *LRAC* curve in which economies of scale and falling long-run average costs give way beyond $SRATC_3$ to diseconomies of scale. $SRATC_3$ represents the lowest unit cost and most **productively efficient** size of firm. This is also sometimes called the optimum size of firm. However, other shapes of *LRAC* curve are also possible. The right-hand panel of Figure 4 shows an L-shaped *LRAC* curve. The size of firm represented by $SRATC_3$ in this diagram is called the **minimum efficient scale (MES)**. It is sited at the point on the *LRAC* curve beyond which no more economies of scale are possible. But there are no diseconomies of scale, so all sizes of firms beyond the *MES* are equally productively efficient.

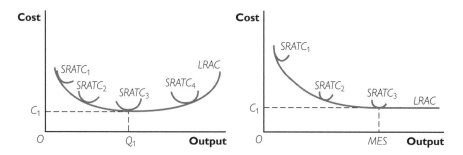

Figure 4 Long-run average cost curves

Examination questions and skills

Examination questions which require detailed explanation of the shape and slope of cost curves are *not* likely to be set. Rather, questions will test your ability to select an appropriate cost curve diagram to use in the explanation, analysis and/or evaluation of, for example, the growth of firms, economies of scale, the nature of production, economic efficiency, and firms' conduct and performance in the different market structures of perfect competition, monopoly and oligopoly.

Common examination errors

Commonly made mistakes on firms, production and costs include the following:
- Assuming that all firms have a single objective — profit maximisation.
- Confusing the short run and the long run, both for production theory and for cost curves.
- Using the long-run concept of economies of scale to explain short-run cost curves.
- Showing no understanding of the relationship between marginal and average costs.
- Badly drawn cost curves, incorrectly labelled with the *MC* curve in the wrong position.
- Confusing marginal and average *returns* with marginal and average *revenue*.
- Writing long irrelevant descriptive answers — for example, on types of economy of scale — when the question requires analysis and the application of theory rather than description.

Market structure and sales revenue

These notes, which relate to AQA specification sections 3.3.1 and 3.3.2, prepare you to answer AQA examination questions on:
- differences between the three market structures of perfect competition, monopoly and oligopoly

content guidance

- revenue curves in perfect competition and monopoly
- the $MR = MC$ rule and profit maximisation

Essential information

Market structures

Whereas cost curves derive from production theory and the cost of hiring the factors of production, a firm's revenue curves depend on the market structure in which it sells its output. Figure 5 shows the main structures recognised by economists.

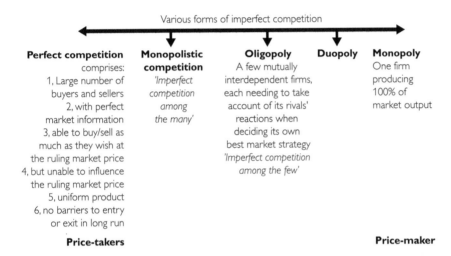

Figure 5 The main market structures

Perfect competition and **monopoly** are at opposite ends of the spectrum shown in Figure 5. In a perfectly competitive market there are a large number of firms. By contrast in monopoly (or strictly **pure monopoly**), a single firm produces the whole of the output of a market or industry. A pure monopolist faces no competition at all, since there are no other firms to compete against. Monopolists do, however, usually face some competitive pressures, both from substitute products and sometimes also from outside firms trying to enter the market to destroy their monopoly position. Pure monopoly is exceedingly rare and often the word 'monopoly' is used in a looser sense to refer to any **highly concentrated market**, in which one firm is dominant.

Every market structure between the extremes of perfect competition and monopoly is a form of **imperfect competition**. There are two main forms of imperfect competition: oligopoly and monopolistic competition. An **oligopoly** is a market dominated by a few large interdependent firms. Interdependence means that an oligopolist has to take account of the likely reactions of the other firms when deciding price and output. **Duopoly** is a special case of oligopoly in which there are just two dominant firms. By contrast to oligopoly, which is sometimes called 'imperfect competition among the few', **monopolistic competition** is 'imperfect competition among the many'. However, monopolistic competition, in which a large number of firms produce goods slightly differentiated by fashion and style, is *not* a part of the AQA specification, so no further mention is made of monopolistic competition in this book.

Perfect competition is an abstract economic model that does not actually exist in any real-world market. This is because the conditions listed in Figure 5 which define perfect competition are too demanding and never occur together simultaneously. Competitive markets in the real world are examples of imperfect competition rather than perfect competition, though some highly competitive markets, such as commodity and financial markets, possess some of the features of perfect competition.

Revenue curves in perfect competition

A perfectly competitive firm's revenue curves are derived from the assumptions, listed in Figure 5, that the firm can sell whatever quantity it wishes at the ruling market price, but that it cannot influence the ruling market price by its own action.

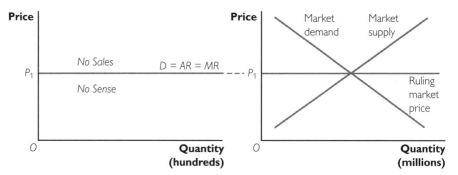

*Figure 6 Deriving the **AR** and **MR** curves of a perfectly competitive firm*

The right-hand panel of Figure 6 shows the whole of a perfectly competitive market, whereas the left-hand panel shows the situation facing a single firm within the market. The ruling market price P_1 is determined in the right-hand panel, where market demand equals market supply. In the left-hand panel of the diagram, each firm faces an infinitely elastic (**perfectly elastic**) demand curve located at P_1, the ruling price set by market forces in the whole market. Consider also the two slogans, 'no sales' and 'no sense', which are respectively above and below P_1. Suppose, first, that the firm tries to set a price above P_1. Possessing perfect market information, the firm's customers immediately stop buying, deciding instead to buy the identical products (which are perfect substitutes) available at P_1 which are produced by other firms in the market — hence 'no sales'. But if the firm can sell as much as it wishes at the ruling price, there is no point in reducing the price below P_1. No extra sales are gained, but the firm loses sales revenue (and profit) — hence 'no sense'. We can conclude that a perfectly competitive firm is a **price-taker**, passively accepting, but unable to influence, the ruling market price.

As well as being the perfectly elastic demand curve for the firm's output, the horizontal line drawn through P_1 is also the perfectly competitive firm's **average revenue (AR)** curve and its **marginal revenue (MR)** curve. Every time it sells one more unit of output, total sales revenue rises by the price at which the extra unit is sold (P_1). Thus marginal revenue is P_1. And because revenue per unit sold is always the same however much is sold, average revenue is P_1 at all levels of output and sales.

Monopoly revenue curves

Monopoly revenue curves differ from those facing a firm in a perfectly competitive market. Because there is only one firm in the market, the market demand curve is the demand curve for the monopolist's output. This means that the monopolist faces a downward-sloping demand curve, whose elasticity is determined by the nature of consumer demand for the monopolist's product. The demand curve can affect the monopolist in one of two different ways. If we regard the monopolist as a **price-maker**, then whenever it sets the price, the demand curve determines how much it can sell. If the monopolist tries to raise the price, it must accept a fall in sales. Alternatively, if the monopolist decides to act as a **quantity setter**, the demand curve dictates the maximum price at which any chosen quantity can be sold. Thus the downward-sloping demand curve means that the monopolist faces a trade-off. A monopoly cannot set price and quantity independently of each other.

Because the demand curve shows the price that the monopolist charges at each level of output, the demand curve is the monopolist's average revenue curve. Unlike perfect competition, however, marginal revenue and average revenue in monopoly are not the same. Because the average revenue curve falls, the marginal revenue curve must be below it. (If you don't understand this, check the explanation of average and marginal curves in the previous topic.) This is illustrated in the left-hand panel of Figure 7. Note that the *MR* curve is twice as steep as the *AR* curve. This is always the case whenever the *AR* curve is both downward sloping and a straight line.

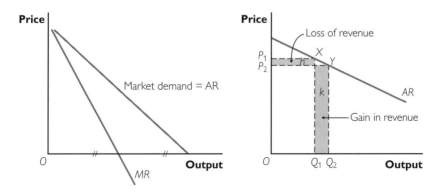

Figure 7 Monopoly average revenue and marginal revenue curves

The relationship between *AR* and *MR* in monopoly can also be explained in another way that is illustrated in the right-hand panel of Figure 7. Because the demand curve (*AR* curve) is downward sloping, the monopolist can sell an extra unit of output only by reducing the price (and average revenue) of all units of output sold. In this situation, total sales revenue *increases* by the shaded area *k* on the diagram, but *decreases* by the shaded area *h*. Area *k* shows a **revenue gain**, namely the extra unit sold multiplied by its price. By contrast, area *h* shows a **revenue loss**. The revenue loss results from the fact that, in order to sell one more unit of output, the price has to be reduced for *all* units of output, not just the extra unit sold. Marginal revenue = the revenue gain *minus* the revenue loss, which must be less than price or average revenue.

The *MR* = *MC* rule and profit maximisation

I noted in the previous topic that economists generally assume that firms have a single objective: profit maximisation. Total profit = total revenue (*TR*) – total cost (*TC*), and a firm aims to produce the level of output at which *TR – TC* is maximised. However, it is often more convenient to state the condition required for profit maximisation as: marginal revenue = marginal cost, or simply *MR* = *MC*.

MR = *MC* means that a firm's profits are greatest when the addition to sales revenue received from the last unit sold (**marginal revenue**) equals exactly the addition to total cost incurred from the production of the last unit of output (**marginal cost**). Consider a farmer producing tomatoes for sale in a local market who is unable to influence the ruling market price of 50p per kilo. At any size of sales, average revenue is 50p, which also equals marginal revenue. Suppose that when the farmer markets 300 kilos of tomatoes, the cost of producing and marketing the 300th kilo is 48p. By deciding not to market the kilo, he sacrifices 2p of profit. Suppose now that total costs rise by 50p and 52p respectively when a 301st kilo and a 302nd kilo are marketed. The marketing of the 302nd kilo causes profits to fall by 2p, but the 301st kilo of tomatoes leaves total profits unchanged: it represents the level of sales at which profits are exactly maximised.

To sum up:
- when MR > MC, profits rise when output and sales increase
- and when MR < MC, profits rise when output and sales fall
- so only when MR = MC are profits maximised

It is important to realise that *MR* = *MC* is the condition for profit maximisation in *all* market structures. In perfect competition, monopoly and oligopoly, profit maximisation occurs only at the level of output and sales at which *MR* = *MC*.

Examination questions and skills

As with cost curves, examination questions which require detailed explanation of the shape and slope of revenue curves are *not* likely to be set. Rather, questions will test your ability to select an appropriate revenue curve diagram to use (probably in conjunction with cost curves) to analyse a particular market structure: perfect competition, monopoly or oligopoly. How to do this is explained in the next four topics.

Common examination errors

Commonly made mistakes on market structure and sales revenue include the following:

- Confusing marginal and average revenue curves with average and marginal returns curves. To avoid this confusion, the latter are best labelled average and marginal product curves.
- Confusing profit maximisation and revenue maximisation.
- Failing to understand the relationship between average and marginal revenue.
- Failing to understand the $MR = MC$ profit-maximising rule, and that it identifies a firm's equilibrium level of output in all market structures: perfect competition, monopoly and oligopoly.
- Writing long, irrelevant answers on the conditions of perfect competition or the causes of monopoly, when the question requires analysis and the application of theory rather than repetition of rote-learnt material.

Perfect competition and monopoly

These notes, which relate to AQA specification sections 3.3.2 and 3.3.3, prepare you to answer AQA examination questions on:

- short-run and long-run equilibrium in perfect competition
- monopoly equilibrium
- causes of monopoly and sources of monopoly power

Essential information

The equilibrium firm

Equilibrium is one of the most important concepts in economics. It means a state of rest or balance, in which there is no reason for anything to change unless it is disturbed, in which case **disequilibrium** replaces equilibrium. You learnt in Unit 1: Markets and Market Failure that a market is in equilibrium when planned demand = planned supply. Within the market, a firm is in equilibrium when it fulfils its market plans. Assuming the firm's sole business objective is profit maximisation, this means it produces and sells the output at which $MR = MC$. If the firm produces below this level of output (in which case $MR > MC$), then, by stepping up output, profit increases. Conversely, if the firm produces beyond the profit-maximising level of output (in which case $MR < MC$), then, by cutting back output, profit increases.

Normal and supernormal profit

Before explaining the profit-maximising or equilibrium firm in perfect competition, it is necessary first to introduce **normal profit** and **supernormal profit**. (Supernormal profit is also known as abnormal profit and above-normal profit.)

Normal profit is the minimum level of profit necessary to keep existing firms in production, while being insufficient to attract new firms into the market. Because a firm must make normal profit to stay in production, economists treat normal profit as a cost of production, including it in a firm's average cost curve. In the long run, firms unable to make normal profit leave the market. Supernormal profit is any extra profit over and above normal profit. In the long run and in the absence of entry barriers, supernormal profit performs the important economic function of attracting new firms into the market.

Perfect competition short-run equilibrium

Figure 8 shows the equilibrium level of output produced by a perfectly competitive firm in the short run. As I explained in the context of the previous topic, the firm (shown in the left-hand panel of the diagram) has to accept the ruling price determined by market supply and demand (shown in the right-hand panel). I also explained that the ruling price is also the firm's average revenue (AR) curve and its marginal revenue (MR) curve. Using the $MR = MC$ condition, the firm's profit-maximising or equilibrium output is Q_1. At Q_1, total sales revenue (quantity sold times price) is shown by the area OP_1YQ_1. Likewise, total cost (quantity sold times average cost) is shown by the area OC_1ZQ_1. This means that the shaded area C_1P_1YZ shows supernormal profit (total revenue minus total cost). Supernormal profit can, of course, be made at levels of output other than Q_1 — indeed, at all levels of output at which price is above average cost. But at these levels of output profit is less than at Q_1. Only by producing and selling Q_1 can the firm make the largest possible supernormal profit.

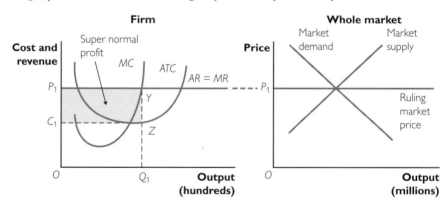

Figure 8 The short-run equilibrium level of output of a perfectly competitive firm

Perfect competition long-run equilibrium

The short-run equilibrium shown in Figure 8 is a temporary equilibrium rather than a true equilibrium. In the short run, new firms cannot enter the market, so incumbent firms (i.e. firms already in the market) continue to make supernormal profit. However in the long run, when there are no entry or exit barriers and firms can enter or leave the market freely, supernormal profit (shown by the shaded area in the left-hand panel of Figure 9) acts as a magnet, attracting new firms into the market. The entry of new firms shifts the market supply curve rightward from S_1 to S_2 in the right-hand panel of Figure 9. This causes the ruling market price to fall until it settles at P_2. Market and firm are now both in long-run or *true* equilibrium.

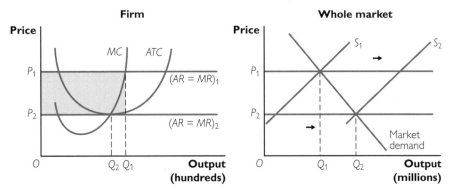

Figure 9 How long-run equilibrium is achieved in perfect competition

Figure 10 shows more clearly a perfectly competitive firm in long-run equilibrium. The price line just touches the lowest point of the firm's *ATC* curve, so no supernormal profit is made. Because the profit made by surviving firms is restricted to normal profit, the incentive for new firms to enter the market no longer exists.

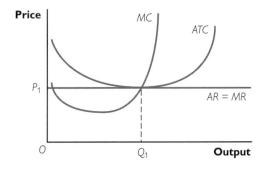

Figure 10 A perfectly competitive firm in long-run equilibrium

Monopoly equilibrium

Just like a perfectly competitive firm, a monopoly maximises profit by producing the level of output at which $MR = MC$. In Figure 11, point A locates the profit-maximising level of output (Q_1). However, the price charged by the monopoly is located at point D on the demand curve (and AR curve), immediately above point A. Supernormal profit (or above-normal profit) is shown by the shaded area C_1P_1DB. Unlike perfect competition, the diagram does not distinguish between *short-run* and *long-run* equilibrium. This is because in monopoly, **entry barriers** prevent new firms joining the market, thus enabling the monopoly to make supernormal profits in the long run as well as the short run. In contrast to perfect competition, where supernormal profits are temporary, a monopoly makes supernormal profit as long as entry barriers protect it. Indeed in monopoly, supernormal profit is often called **monopoly profit**, indicating the monopolist's power to preserve profit by preventing competition.

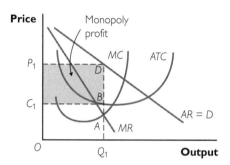

Figure 11 Monopoly equilibrium

Causes of monopoly and sources of monopoly power

Monopoly power stems from a firm's ability to exclude rivals from the market by imposing entry barriers. A pure monopoly obviously possesses monopoly power, but firms in imperfectly competitive markets such as oligopolies can also exercise monopoly power to a greater or lesser extent. Whereas perfect competition is characterised by **consumer sovereignty** (in the sense that firms respond to the wishes of consumers exercised through their pounds spent in the market), monopolies exercise and exploit **producer sovereignty**. Consumers cannot go elsewhere to buy the good, and are presented with a 'take it or leave it' choice. Enjoying producer sovereignty, a firm with monopoly power exploits consumers by restricting output and raising price by restricting consumer choice and by making permanent excess profit.

But even when a firm is a monopoly producer of a particular good or service, monopoly power is weak if close substitutes exist, produced by other firms in other industries. Monopoly power is greatest when the firm produces an essential good for which there are no substitutes. Factors that give rise to monopoly power include advantages of geographical location, control over raw material supply or market outlets, economies of scale, the use of advertising, branding and product differentiation as entry barriers, and laws such as patent legislation, which protect innovations and intellectual property from copying.

Natural monopoly

In the past, utility industries such as water, gas, electricity and the telephone industry possessed great monopoly power. Because of the nature of their product, utility industries experience a particular marketing problem. The industries produce a service that is delivered through a distribution network or grid of pipes and cables into millions of separate businesses and homes. Competition in the provision of distribution grids is extremely wasteful, since it requires the duplication of fixed capacity, therefore causing each supplier to incur unnecessarily high fixed costs. For this reason, the utility industries were said to be natural monopolies: that is, industries that would be monopolies whoever owned them. Until the 1980s and 1990s, most UK utilities such as the British Gas Corporation and BT were publicly owned monopolies and nationalised industries. Virtually all the utilities have now been privatised. The topic 'Industrial policy' (pp. 42–47) looks at how regulation and deregulation are used to remove entry barriers and make the utility markets competitive and contestable.

Examination questions and skills

Examination questions, usually part (1) of essay questions, are likely to test the skill of explaining and illustrating profit maximisation in perfect competition and/or monopoly. The command word in part (1) of an essay question is *explain*. By contrast, part (2) asks you to *evaluate*, *assess* or *discuss*. You might be asked to evaluate the desirable and undesirable properties of perfect competition equilibrium and/or monopoly equilibrium. The skills needed, which relate to efficiency concepts, are explained in the topic 'Evaluating market structures' (pp. 36–41).

Common examination errors

Commonly made mistakes on perfect competition and monopoly include the following:
- Explaining perfect competition equilibrium solely in terms of the whole market and not a firm within the market, or vice versa.
- Failing to apply correctly the $MR = MC$ rule, particularly for monopoly equilibrium.
- Failing to distinguish between short-run and long-run equilibrium in perfect competition.
- Failing to understand normal profit and supernormal profit and to apply the concepts in analysis.
- Writing long irrelevant answers on the causes of monopoly, when the question requires explanation, analysis and evaluation of monopoly equilibrium.

Oligopoly

These notes, which relate to AQA specification section 3.3.3, prepare you to answer AQA examination questions on:
- the meaning of oligopoly
- competitive and collusive oligopoly
- different ways in which prices are set in imperfectly competitive markets

Essential information

The meaning of oligopoly

Oligopoly is a market structure in which a few large firms dominate the market. This means there is a high degree of market concentration, which can be measured by a **concentration ratio**. For example, a five-firm concentration ratio of 80% means that the five largest firms produce 80% of market output.

However, oligopoly is best defined by the *behaviour* of the firms within the market, rather than by market *structure*. Oligopolists are *interdependent* rather than *independent*, in the sense that they need to take account of the likely reactions of their rivals, the other oligopolists, when making price and output decisions. Consider, for example, an oligopolist who is thinking of raising the price charged in order to increase profit. Whether the price rise succeeds in increasing profit depends upon the likely reactions of the other firms. Will rival firms follow suit and match the price rise, or will they hold their prices steady, hoping to gain sales at the expense of the firm that raised the price? Clearly, when deciding whether to raise or lower its price, an oligopolist must make assumptions about the likely response of the other firms.

Because there are a very great number of possible ways in which oligopolistic firms may react to each other's pricing and output strategies, it is impossible to construct an all-embracing oligopoly theory. The more sophisticated oligopoly models are examples of **game theory**. Each oligopolist is regarded as a player in a game, choosing a strategy to win the game by attaching statistical probabilities to various possible outcomes and to the likely retaliatory strategies adopted by its rivals. Different assumptions about the likely reaction of rivals may lead to a different pricing decision by the firm itself.

Perfect and imperfect oligopoly

Perfect oligopoly exists when the oligopolists produce a uniform or homogeneous product such as petrol. By contrast, imperfect oligopoly occurs when the products of the oligopoly are by their nature differentiated, such as automobiles.

Competitive and collusive oligopoly

As I have noted, in competitive oligopoly a firm has to take account of the reactions of its rivals when forming its market strategy, but it does so without cooperating or colluding with the other firms. Uncertainty is a characteristic of competitive oligopoly — a firm can never be completely certain of how rivals will react to its marketing strategy. Will they or will they not follow suit?

Uncertainty can be reduced by the rivals cooperating or colluding to fix prices or output, or even by allocating customers to particular members of the oligopoly. For example, by forming a **cartel agreement** or **price ring**, oligopolists can achieve a better outcome for them all, in terms of **joint-profit maximisation** and an easier life, than by remaining a competitive oligopoly. However, collusion or cooperative behaviour may not be good for the consumer, resulting in the disadvantages of monopoly, such as high prices and restriction of choice, without any of the benefits, such as economies of scale. For this reason, collusive oligopolistic arrangements such as cartel agreements are normally illegal, regarded by governments as against the public interest. In any case, it is seldom possible to eliminate uncertainty completely. Members of a cartel may cheat or renege on an agreement, secretly selling extra output at a price that undercuts the cartel's agreed price.

The kinked demand curve theory of competitive oligopoly

The kinked demand curve theory, which is illustrated in Figure 12, can be used to explain a number of features of competitive oligopoly, such as interdependence, uncertainty and a preference for avoiding price wars. The theory was originally developed to explain price rigidity and the absence of price wars in oligopolistic markets. Suppose an oligopolist sells output Q_1 at price P_1 as shown in the left-hand panel of Figure 12. Because oligopolists lack accurate information about the demand and revenue curves they face, particularly at outputs other than those they are currently producing, each firm has to guess what will happen to demand if it changes its price.

The demand curve DD in Figure 12 represents an oligopolist's estimate of how demand will change with respect to either a price rise or a price fall. DD has been drawn on the assumption that the firm expects demand for its product to be relatively elastic in response to a price rise because rivals are expected to react by keeping their prices stable in the hope of gaining profits and market share. But the oligopolist expects demand to be relatively inelastic when the price is cut. This is because the oligopolist expects rivals to react to a price cut by decreasing their prices by the same amount. Few, if any, customers are likely to be lured away from rival firms.

The oligopolist therefore expects rival firms to react asymmetrically when price is raised compared to when price is lowered. The oligopolist's initial price and output, P_1 and Q_1, are located at the junction of two demand curves with different elasticities, each curve reflecting a different assumption about how rivals are expected to react to a change in price. The oligopolist expects profit to be lost whether price is raised or cut. On these assumptions, the best policy is to leave price unchanged.

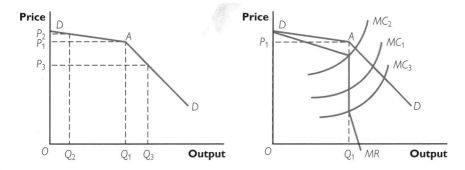

Figure 12 The kinked demand curve theory

The right-hand panel of Figure 12 illustrates a way in which the kinked demand curve theory can be developed further. As in all market structures, the demand curve facing an oligopolist is also its average revenue (AR) curve. But as we saw for monopoly in the topic 'Perfect competition and monopoly' (pp. 27–31), when AR falls, marginal revenue (MR) is below AR. You should note that the MR curve in Figure 12 has three sections. The uppermost section relates to the more elastic section of the AR curve to the left of the kink at point A, while the lowermost section relates to the less elastic section of the AR curve below and to the right of the kink. The mid-section of the MR curve is the vertical line joining the upper and lower sections of the MR curve below point A at the output level Q_1. Suppose the MC curve is initially MC_1. Since MR = MC at this level of output, P_1 must be the profit-maximising price. However, if marginal cost rises or falls between MC_2 and MC_3, the profit-maximising output and price continue respectively to be Q_1 and P_1. The oligopolist's selling price remains stable despite quite significant changes in costs of production.

Weaknesses of the kinked demand curve theory

Although at first sight attractive as an explanation of price stability in conditions of oligopoly, the kinked demand theory has two significant weaknesses. First, it is an incomplete theory, since it does not explain how and why a firm chooses to be at point A in the first place. Second, evidence provided by the pricing decisions of real-world firms gives little support to the theory. Rival firms seldom respond to price changes in the manner assumed in the kinked demand curve theory, and it is also reasonable to expect that an oligopolist would test the market: that is, raise or lower the selling price to see if rivals react in the manner expected. If the rivals did not, then the oligopolist would surely revise its estimate of demand for its product. Evidence conclusively shows that oligopoly prices tend to be stable or sticky when demand conditions change in a predictable or cyclical way, and that oligopolists usually raise or lower prices quickly and by significant amounts, both when production costs change substantially and when unexpected shifts in demand occur.

Non-price competition

The kinked demand curve theory suggests that oligopolists are reluctant to use **price competition** to gain sales and market share, although there is plenty of evidence that oligopolists do on occasion engage in **price wars**, even though, according to the kinked demand theory, such wars are self-defeating. Nevertheless, oligopolists also engage in many forms of **non-price competition**, such as marketing competition (for example, obtaining exclusive outlets such as tied public houses and petrol stations through which breweries and oil companies can sell their products), the use of persuasive advertising, product differentiation, brand imaging and packaging, and quality competition, including the provision of after-sales service.

Price discrimination

Oligopolists (and monopolists) sometimes use price discrimination to increase their profits. Price discrimination occurs when firms charge different prices to different customers based on differences in the customers' ability and willingness to pay. Those customers who are prepared to pay more are charged a higher price than those who are only willing to pay a lower price. It is important to understand that discriminatory prices are for the most part based on differences in demand conditions rather than on differences in costs of production. You should refer to the answer to part (1) of the second essay question in the Questions and Answers section of this guide for further explanation of price discrimination.

Other aspects of pricing in imperfect competition

Imperfectly competitive firms (and also monopolies) set prices in several different ways.

- **Cost-plus pricing**, also known as mark-up pricing and full-cost pricing, is a commonly used pricing rule. Cost-plus pricing means that a firm sets its selling price by adding a standard percentage profit margin to average or unit costs.
- **Price leadership** is also common in oligopoly, perhaps because overt collusive agreements to fix the market price, such as cartel agreements, are usually illegal. Price leadership occurs when one firm becomes the market leader and other firms in the industry follow its pricing example.
- **Limit pricing** and **predatory pricing** are two forms of pricing undertaken by dominant firms in markets where natural entry barriers are low or non-existent. In the case of limit pricing, a dominant firm realises that if it sets the short-run profit-maximising price, the entry of new firms will quickly erode its supernormal profit. To prevent this happening, the dominant firm sets a deliberately low price (the limit price) to deter entry by new firms. The firm sacrifices short-term profits that a higher price would yield in order to maximise long-run profits, achieved through preventing or limiting the entry of new firms. Limit pricing, which is legal, is related to the theory of contestable markets (see the topic 'Industrial policy', pp. 42–47). In contrast to limit pricing, which deters market entry, successful predatory pricing removes recent entrants to the market. Predatory pricing occurs when an incumbent firm deliberately sets prices below cost to force new market entrants out of business. Once the new entrants have left the market and its dominance has been restored, the firm will restore prices to their previous profit-maximising level. Predatory pricing is an anti-competitive trading restrictive practice (see the section 'Industrial policy'), and is therefore illegal.

Examination questions and skills

Virtually every real-world market is imperfectly competitive, so it is easy for principal examiners to find source material on oligopoly that is suitable for a data-response question. The global context DRQ 2 on General Motors and Vauxhall Motors in the Questions and Answers section of this guide is an example.

The kinked demand curve theory is unlikely to figure explicitly in a question. Questions will, however, be set on the behaviour of oligopolistic firms. If properly used and applied, the kinked demand curve theory can be used to explain and analyse many aspects of competitive oligopoly: for example, how firms are affected by interdependence and uncertainty, and why oligopolists may prefer non-price competition to price competition.

Common examination errors

Commonly made mistakes on oligopoly include the following:

- Imprecise descriptions of market structure and concentration.
- Defining oligopoly solely in terms of market structure rather than the firms' interdependence.
- Failing to understand why oligopolists may wish to collude.
- Inaccurately drawn diagrams and inaccurate written explanation of the kinked demand curve theory.
- Failing to understand the theory of price discrimination.
- Writing all the candidate knows about the kinked demand curve theory, when the question requires selective application of theory to the issue posed by the question.

Evaluating market structures

These notes, which relate to AQA specification section 3.3.3, prepare you to answer AQA examination questions on applying:

- efficiency concepts to evaluate market structures
- welfare concepts to evaluate market structures

Essential information

The meaning of economic efficiency

Any economic decision or course of action (by an individual, a firm or the government) is *efficient* if it achieves the economic agent's desired objective at minimum cost to the agent, and with minimum undesired side-effects or distortion. More specifically, how well or badly a market performs depends in part on its *efficiency*. A number of different efficiency concepts are used to evaluate market performance. Those in the Unit 3 specification are **productive efficiency, allocative efficiency, static efficiency** and **dynamic efficiency**. Although not in the specification (and therefore not figuring explicitly in Unit 3 examination questions), two other efficiency concepts will be considered: **technical efficiency** and **X-efficiency**.

Technical efficiency

A production process is technically efficient if it *maximises* the output of a good produced from given or available inputs. Alternatively, it can be said that for a particular level of output, a production process is technically efficient if it *minimises* the inputs of capital and labour required to produce that level of output.

Productive efficiency

Whereas technical efficiency is defined in terms of the relationship in production between inputs and outputs, productive efficiency (cost efficiency) is usually measured in terms of money costs of production. Productive efficiency requires that output is produced at the lowest possible average cost. In the *short run*, the productively-efficient level of output occurs at the lowest point on the firm's short-run *ATC* curve. For the firm shown in Figure 13, this is output Q_1, where average costs are minimised at C_1.

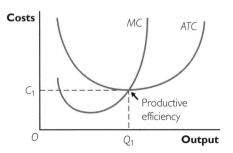

Figure 13 Productive efficiency

But in the *long run*, the most productively efficient of *all* the firm's possible levels of output is produced at the lowest point on the firm's long-run average cost (*LRAC*) curve, at the scale or size of firm that minimises unit costs. Remember also that the economy as a whole is productively efficient — and also technically efficient — when it is producing on its production possibility frontier.

X-efficiency

X-inefficiency occurs whenever, for any particular scale of fixed capacity and level of production, the firm incurs unnecessary production costs: that is, it could in principle reduce costs. There are two causes of X-inefficiency: combining factors of production in a technically inefficient way to produce a particular level of output (for example, over-manning and continuously idle machinery); and paying workers or managers unnecessarily high wages or salaries, or buying raw materials or capital at unnecessarily high prices. A firm is producing X-efficiently when, given its size or available capacity, it eliminates all unnecessary costs of production. The firm shown in Figure 14 is X-inefficient if it produces output Q_1 at an average cost of C_2 (that is, the firm is producing *above* its average cost curve at point X). By contrast, if the firm produces *on* its average cost curve (at C_1), it is X-efficient. All points on the *ATC* curve are X-efficient.

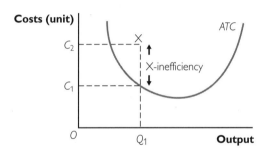

Figure 14 X-efficiency and X-inefficiency

Allocative efficiency

Allocative efficiency relates to how the goods produced from the economy's scarce resources are used: that is, how they are allocated between final uses. As a generalisation, allocative efficiency occurs when the goods and services produced match people's needs and preferences. More specifically, an economy is said to be allocatively efficient when it is impossible to allocate final goods so as to make one person better off without at the same time making another person worse off. A necessary condition for a market economy to be allocatively efficient is that the prices of all goods must equal their marginal costs of production: $P = MC$ throughout the economy. A particular market is allocatively efficient if, in that market, $P = MC$. Strictly however, prices must also equal relevant marginal costs in all other markets in the economy.

Static efficiency

All the efficiency types considered so far are forms of static efficiency. Static efficiency side-steps the fact that the economy is constantly changing, with new technologies, methods of production and final goods being developed and economic growth taking place.

Dynamic efficiency

In contrast to static efficiency, dynamic efficiency results from improvements in technical and productive efficiency occurring over time. A dynamically efficient economy is proficient at improving methods of producing existing products, and also at developing and marketing completely new products. Dynamic efficiency should be linked to the emphasis in the specification on the ways in which **technical progress** affects market structure. It is important to understand how invention, innovation, research and development (R & D) and **technological change** impact upon methods and costs of production, and on productive and dynamic efficiency.

Evaluating perfect competition and monopoly in terms of economic efficiency

The left-hand and right-hand panels of Figure 15 respectively show a perfectly competitive firm and a monopoly in equilibrium — assuming that firms in both markets have similar *ATC* curves. This means there are no **economies of scale**. The diagram shows that the perfectly competitive firm is productively efficient (producing where *ATC* is lowest), but that monopoly is productively inefficient (producing above minimum *ATC*). Likewise, the perfectly competitive firm is allocatively efficient (as $P = MC$), whereas the monopoly is allocatively inefficient (since $P > MC$). Compared to perfect competition, the monopoly's price is too high and its output is too low.

In long-run equilibrium, a perfectly competitive firm must also be X-efficient. The reason is simple. If the firm is X-inefficient, incurring unnecessary costs, the firm could not make normal profits in the long run. To survive or make normal profits, the firm must take action to eliminate organisational slack or X-inefficiency. Because of the absence of competitive pressures, which in perfect competition serve to eliminate supernormal profit, monopoly may also be X-inefficient. A monopoly can often survive, happily incurring unnecessary production costs and making *satisfactory* rather than *maximum* profits, because the absence or weakness of competitive forces means that there is no mechanism in monopoly to eliminate X-inefficiency.

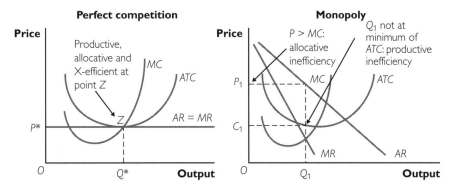

Figure 15 Evaluating perfect competition and monopoly in terms of economic efficiency

However, the conclusion that perfect competition is productively more efficient than monopoly depends on an assumption that there are no economies of scale. When substantial economies of scale are possible in an industry, monopoly may be productively more efficient than competition. Figure 16 illustrates a natural monopoly where, because of limited market size, there is no room in the market for more than one firm benefiting from full economies of scale. Producing on the short-run average cost curve $SRATC_N$, the monopoly may be producing above the lowest point on this particular cost curve, hence exhibiting a degree of productive inefficiency. However, *all* points drawn on $SRATC_N$ incur lower unit costs — and are productively *more* efficient — than any point on $SRATC_1$, which is the relevant cost curve for each firm if the monopoly is broken into a number of smaller competitive enterprises.

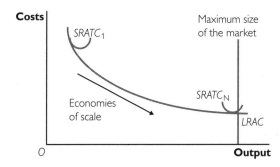

Figure 16 The justification of monopoly when economies of scale are possible

Under certain circumstances, monopolies may also be more **dynamically efficient** than a perfectly competitive firm. Because it is protected by entry barriers, a monopoly earns monopoly profit without facing the threat that the profit will be whittled away as new firms enter the market. This allows an innovating monopoly to enjoy the fruits of successful R & D and product development in the form of monopoly profit. In perfect competition, by contrast, there is little or no incentive to innovate because other firms can 'free ride' and gain costless access to the results of any successful research. This argument is used to justify **patent legislation**, which grants a firm the right to exploit the monopoly position created by innovation for a number of years before the patent expires.

However, there is a counter-argument, namely that monopoly reduces rather than promotes innovation and dynamic efficiency. As I mentioned earlier, protected from competitive pressures, a monopoly may *profit satisfice* rather than *profit maximise*, content with satisfactory profits and an easy life.

Evaluating perfect competition and monopoly in terms of economic welfare

To explain how market structures affect economic welfare, I must first introduce the concepts of consumer surplus and producer surplus as measures of welfare. Consumer surplus and producer surplus are illustrated in Figure 17.

Consumer surplus is the difference between the *maximum* price a consumer is prepared to pay and the *actual* price he or she need pay. In a competitive market such as the left-hand side of Figure 17, the total consumer surplus enjoyed by all the consumers in the market is measured by the triangular area P_1EA. Consumer welfare increases whenever consumer surplus increases: for example, when market prices fall. Conversely, however, higher prices reduce consumer surplus and welfare.

Producer surplus, which is a measure of producers' welfare, is the difference between the *minimum price* a firm is prepared to charge for a good and the *actual price* charged. In the left-hand side of Figure 17, the producer surplus enjoyed by all the firms in the market is measured by the triangular area FP_1A.

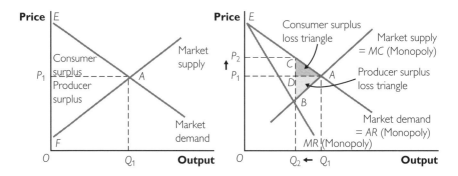

Figure 17 Market structure and economic welfare

The right-hand side of Figure 17 illustrates what happens to economic welfare when monopoly replaces perfect competition (assuming there are no economies of scale). Market equilibrium in perfect competition is determined at point A: output is Q_1 and price is P_1. Monopoly equilibrium, by contrast, is determined at point B, where $MR = MC$. (Note that the marginal cost curve in monopoly is the same curve as market supply in perfect competition.) The diagram illustrates the standard case against monopoly, namely that compared to perfect competition, monopoly restricts output (to Q_2) and raises price (to P_2). But I can now take the analysis one stage further and investigate how consumer surplus and producer surplus (and hence economic welfare) are affected. Raising the price from P_1 to P_2 transfers consumer surplus away from consumers and to the monopoly. The transfer is shown by the rectangle bounded by the points P_1P_2C and D. Producer surplus (in the form of monopoly profit) increases at the expense of consumer surplus. Over and above this transfer, there is also a **net loss of economic welfare** caused by the fact that the amount bought and sold falls to Q_2. The welfare loss (**deadweight loss**) is shown by the two shaded triangular areas in the right-hand panel of Figure 17. The upper triangle shows a loss of consumer surplus and the lower triangle shows a similar loss of producer surplus.

Examination questions and skills

In this topic I have explained economic efficiency and economic welfare in the context of the two extreme market structures of perfect competition and monopoly. Exam questions might also require efficiency and/or welfare concepts to be used to explain, analyse and evaluate firms' behaviour and performance in imperfectly competitive markets lying between the two extreme market structures. For example, welfare loss (and transfer of consumer surplus) is relevant to part (1) of EQ2 on price discrimination.

Common examination errors

Commonly made mistakes on evaluating market structures include the following:
- Confusing the different types of economic efficiency.
- Failing to understand allocative efficiency.
- Confusing efficiency with equity.
- Inability to apply efficiency concepts to analyse the properties of profit-maximising firms in perfect competition and monopoly.
- Wrongly arguing that perfect competition is efficient and monopoly is inefficient because entrepreneurs in perfectly competitive markets take account of the public interest and do not pursue their private self-interests.
- Failing to appreciate the economies of scale and dynamic efficiency justifications of monopoly.
- Failing to understand and apply the concepts of economic welfare, consumer surplus and producer surplus.

Industrial policy

These notes, which relate to AQA specification section 3.3.5, prepare you to answer AQA examination questions on:

- competition policy
- public ownership and privatisation
- regulation and deregulation of markets

Essential information

Industrial policy and competition policy

Industrial policy is part of the government's **microeconomic policy** that aims to improve the economic performance of individual economic agents, firms and industries on the supply side of the economy. Industrial policy therefore provides examples of microeconomic **supply-side economic policies**.

Since its beginnings in 1948, competition policy has been an important part of UK industrial policy. Competition policy is the part of industrial policy that covers **monopolies**, **mergers** and **restrictive trading practices**.

Monopoly policy

UK policy identifies two types of monopoly known as scale monopoly and complex monopoly. **Scale monopoly** occurs when one firm has at least 25% of the market, whereas a **complex monopoly** exists when a number of firms together have a 25% share and conduct their affairs so as to restrict competition.

By comparison to perfect competition, monopoly may reduce output and raise prices, thus promoting productive and allocative inefficiency. Monopolies may also exploit their producer sovereignty by manipulating consumer wants and restricting choice, and by **price discriminating** between different groups of customers. However, the key argument against monopoly — that dominant firms use market power to restrict output and raise prices — depends crucially upon the assumption that firms of different size all have similar cost curves. In industries where **economies of large-scale production** are possible, this is not the case. The existence of economies of scale means that large firms can benefit from lower costs and achieve a more productively efficient outcome than smaller firms, and monopolies may also be more dynamically efficient.

In the past, **utility industries** such as gas, water and electricity supply, sewage disposal, telecommunications and postal services were regarded as natural monopolies. The key question was: should natural monopolies be organised as **nationalised industries**, or should they be left in private hands, but subject to strong and effective government **regulation**?

UK competition policy has generally recognised that monopoly can be good or bad, depending upon circumstances. It has adopted the pragmatic view that each case of monopoly must be judged on its merits. If the likely costs resulting from the reduction of competition exceed the benefits, monopoly should be prevented. But if the likely benefits exceed the costs, monopoly should be permitted, provided the monopoly does not abuse its position and exploit the consuming public.

UK monopoly policy is implemented by the Office of Fair Trading (OFT) and the Competition Commission, which are responsible to a government ministry, the Department for Business, Innovation and Skills (BIS). The OFT uses market structure, conduct and performance indicators to scan or screen the UK economy on a systematic basis for evidence of monopoly abuse. Concentration ratios provide evidence of monopolistic market structures, while market conduct indicators, such as consumer and trade complaints and evidence of price discrimination, price leadership and merger activity, allow the OFT to monitor anti-competitive business behaviour. The performance indicators used to measure business efficiency include price movements and changes in profit margins.

When the OFT discovers evidence of statutory monopoly which it believes is likely to be against the public interest, it refers the firms involved to the Competition Commission for further investigation. The Competition Commission interprets the public interest largely in terms of the effect upon competitiveness of the trading practices it is asked to investigate. Following an investigation, the Competition Commission reports its findings to the Department for Business, Innovation and Skills, which may then: implement some or all of the recommendations; shelve the report and do nothing; or take action completely contrary to the commission's advice.

In fact, the government has quite wide powers to take action on receipt of the Competition Commission's recommendations. In extreme cases, the government can issue an order requiring firms to split up or sell off assets. In practice, however, these order-making powers are seldom used.

Although a **cost–benefit** approach which involves taking each case on its merits is central to UK monopoly policy, there are a number of other possible approaches to the problems posed by monopoly. These include the following:

- **The compulsory breaking up of all monopolies**. Some economists believe that only when the economy resembles perfect competition will the advantages of a free-market economy, namely economic efficiency and consumer sovereignty, be achieved. Monopoly must be regarded as bad and can never be justified. This approach suggests the adoption of an automatic policy rule to break up existing monopolies.
- **Price controls**. These are used in the form of the **RPI–X price cap** imposed on privatised utility companies such as BT.
- **Taxing monopoly profits.** This is to encourage monopolies to reduce prices and profits.
- **Public ownership**. Labour governments have sometimes regarded the problem of monopoly as resulting from private ownership and the pursuit of private profit. They nationalised monopolies in the belief that state-owned monopolies act in the public interest.

- **Privatisation**. In contrast to the socialist view that the problem of monopoly stems in large part from private ownership and the profit motive, free-market economists believe that state ownership produces abuses, such as a feather-bedded workforce protected from any form of market discipline. They argue that privatisation improves efficiency and commercial performance because it exposes firms to the threat of takeover and market discipline.
- **Removing barriers to entry**. Privatisation alone cannot end monopoly abuse, since it merely changes the nature of the problem back to private monopoly and the commercial exploitation of a monopoly position. Entry barriers must also be removed to make the market contestable.

A market is contestable if the potential exists for firms to enter and leave the market without incurring entry or exit costs. In particular, there must be no or few sunk costs. Sunk costs are costs incurred when a firm enters a market, which it cannot recover if it decides to leave. Huge sums spent on advertising and promotion, which are irrecoverable if the firm fails to penetrate the market and decides to cut its losses and leave, are a sunk cost. A complete absence of sunk costs and entry barriers means that a market is perfectly contestable. Such markets may attract hit-and-run entrants: that is, new firms that enter the market, make a quick profit and then leave.

Modern monopoly policy centres on making markets contestable by removing entry and exit barriers and trying to reduce sunk costs. Actual contestability is not required, only **potential contestability**. A dominant firm may survive in a contestable market by setting **limit prices** (see p. 35).

The theory of contestable markets suggests that monopoly should be defined, not by the number of firms in the market or by concentration ratios, but rather by the potential ease or difficulty with which new firms may enter the market. Monopoly should not be regarded as a problem, even if there is only one established firm in the market, providing that an absence of barriers to entry and exit creates the *potential* for new firms to enter and contest the market. This is sufficient, according to the contestable market theory, to ensure efficient and non-exploitative behaviour by existing firms within the market. Government intervention should be restricted to discovering which industries and markets are potentially contestable, and then using **regulatory** and **deregulatory policies** to develop conditions, through the removal of barriers to entry and exit, to ensure that contestability is possible.

Merger policy

Merger policy is concerned with takeovers and acquisitions that might create a monopoly situation. As with the part of competition policy that deals with already established monopolies and concentrated markets, UK merger policy reflects the influence of **contestable market theory**. Currently a merger is only usually referred for investigation by the Competition Commission if the OFT believes the merger might have significant anti-competitive effects. Lateral or diversifying mergers or takeovers are not usually investigated, nor are takeovers by overseas-based multinational companies.

Critics believe that UK merger policy is much too weak and ineffective. However, the ability of a UK government to toughen its merger policy is limited by the fact that many mergers involving UK companies fall under the remit of European Union competition policy. Under the EU principle of **subsidiarity**, which delegates policy as much as possible to national governments, UK national policy deals with smaller mergers, but the European Commission adjudicates on larger mergers with an EU dimension.

Policy towards restrictive trading practices

Restrictive trading practices undertaken by firms in imperfectly competitive markets divide into those undertaken independently by a single firm, and collective restrictive practices that involve an agreement or collusion between two or more firms. The former include refusal to supply and full-line forcing, whereby a supplier forces a distributor that wishes to sell one of the supplier's products to stock the full range of its products. Such practices are often considered as evidence of anti-competitive market conduct or behaviour when the OFT decides on monopoly references. By contrast, **collective restrictive agreements and practices**, such as **cartel agreements** (price rings), when discovered, are referred by the OFT to a court of law, the **Restrictive Practice Court (RPC)**. The RPC has the full power and independence of a high court. Firms found guilty of illegal collusion are fined, though not as heavily as when they fall foul of EU cartel policy. Many economists believe that UK policy towards anti-competitive restrictive trading practices should be made much tougher.

Not all collective agreements and acts of collusion between firms are anti-competitive and against the public interest. **Collective training schemes** for workers and jointly undertaken research and development (R & D) respectively lead to better human and non-human capital, thereby contributing to improvements in dynamic efficiency.

Public ownership and privatisation

In the past, industries have been **nationalised** (taken into public ownership) to deal with the problem of natural monopoly and to give the government control of the key industries, deemed vital for the planning of the economy. The 1950s to the 1970s were the decades of the **mixed economy**, when the major political parties agreed that a mix of public and private enterprise worked and was right for the UK. But this consensus broke down around 1980, and since then, successive UK governments have generally followed a policy of **economic liberalisation**, two of whose elements are **privatisation** and **deregulation**.

Privatisation involves the transfer of ownership, usually by sale, of industries and other assets from the public sector to the private sector. Free-market economists believe that by exposing firms and industries to the discipline of the market (the capital market as well as the market in which the privatised firm sells its output), privatisation improves efficiency and economic performance. Free-marketers also argue that, by extending share ownership to individuals and employees, privatisation promotes popular capitalism and an enterprise culture. Privatisation also raises revenue for the government, which reduces, at least in the short run, the government's need to borrow.

Deregulation is the opposite of regulation. Regulation restricts economic agents' freedom of action in the marketplace. By removing previously imposed rules and constraints, deregulation increases people's freedom to pursue their self-interest. Free-market economists argue that many regulations are unnecessary, creating bureaucracy and 'red tape', which raise business costs and render firms uncompetitive. Regulation can also be an entry barrier, protecting the monopoly power of firms already in the market. Finally, regulation can lead to a process known as **regulatory capture**. Regulatory capture allegedly occurs when a regulator (for example, an agency regulating a privatised utility industry) 'goes native' and acts in the interest of the powerful firms that it is supposed to constrain, rather than in the interest of the consumers that it is meant to protect. Nevertheless, many regulations — for example, health and safety regulations — are undoubtedly necessary. Great harm would occur if *all* regulations and protective laws were abolished or repealed.

Other policies of economic liberalisation used in conjunction with privatisation and deregulation include contractualisation, competitive tendering, the private finance initiative and marketisation. **Contractualisation**, which is closely related to privatisation, occurs when public sector organisations such as NHS hospitals contract out the provision of services such as catering to private sector firms. The taxpayer may still pick up the bill, but private sector firms provide the service. **Competitive tendering** goes one stage further. Private sector firms tender (that is, compete) for public sector business and contracts are awarded to the firms that appear to offer best value for money. Under the **private finance initiative (PFI)**, part of the cost of major public sector investment projects is financed by the private sector, thereby saving taxpayers' money (at least in the short term). **Marketisation** (commercialisation) switches the provision of goods or services from the non-market sector (financed by taxation) to the market sector (financed by sales revenue). Do not confuse *marketisation* with *privatisation*, which switches provision from the public sector to the private sector.

Examination questions and skills

European Union context data-response questions might be set, testing knowledge of the fact that mergers and takeovers involving businesses that trade in the UK may be subject to EU competition law as well as to UK national law. Essay questions may focus on the topics of public ownership, privatisation and regulation and deregulation, in the context of monopoly, oligopoly and price setting and contestable market theory.

Common examination errors

Commonly made mistakes on industrial policy include the following:

- Confusing scale monopoly (25% of the market) with pure monopoly (100% of the market).
- Writing a historical account of UK competition policy rather than analysing and evaluating the effectiveness of current policy.
- Failing to appreciate the cost–benefit approach of UK monopoly policy.
- Lack of awareness of alternative approaches to the problems posed by monopolies and market concentration.
- Confusing policy towards established monopoly with policy towards mergers that might create a new monopoly.
- Writing a historical account of UK privatisation rather than analysing and evaluating the advantages and disadvantages of privatisation and/or the track record of a privatised industry.
- Confusing privatisation with related policies such as marketisation and deregulation.

Market failure, government failure and cost–benefit analysis

These notes, which relate to AQA specification section 3.3.5, prepare you to answer AQA examination questions on:

- market failure
- government failure
- cost–benefit analysis

Essential information

AS and A2 specification coverage of market failure

Market failure and **government failure** feature in both the AS Unit 1 and the A2 Unit 3 specifications. These notes focus on the extra knowledge and understanding required by the Unit 3 specification. They repeat only selectively the basic knowledge that the Unit 1: Markets and Market Failure examination assesses. You should refer back to the Unit 1 Guide, pp. 29–33, to refresh this knowledge, especially with regard to the marginal private, external and social cost and benefit diagrams used to illustrate some of the main market failures, namely externalities and merit goods and demerit goods.

The meaning of market failure

Market failure occurs whenever the market mechanism or price mechanism performs unsatisfactorily. Sometimes markets perform **inequitably**: for example, when unregulated market forces produce extreme inequalities in the distributions of income and wealth, which most people would deem unfair or unjust. The other market failures you are expected to know result from the market mechanism performing **inefficiently**.

Market failure and allocative efficiency

Much of the extra knowledge and understanding required for the Unit 3 exam centres on the concepts of allocative efficiency (and inefficiency) and property rights. This section of notes explains the significance of allocative efficiency, while property rights are covered in the next section.

I have already explained (on pages 38–39) how **monopoly** may lead to market failure because the monopoly sets a price above the marginal cost of production ($P > MC$). The price is too high and too little is produced. As well as being productively inefficient (assuming no economies of scale), monopoly is allocatively inefficient.

You learnt at AS how **public goods** such as national defence possess the twin characteristics of **non-excludability** and **non-rivalry**. Non-rivalry (which is also known as **non-diminishability** and **non-exhaustibility**) means that whenever an extra person consumes a public good, the benefits available to other people are not reduced. As a result, the marginal cost of providing the good to an extra user is zero. As allocative efficiency requires that $P = MC$, the allocatively efficient level of consumption of a public good occurs when $P = 0$. But market provision requires $P > 0$ to create a market-based incentive, namely profit, for entrepreneurs to provide the good. If $P > 0$, the price charged must also be greater than marginal cost ($P > MC$), which is allocatively inefficient, resulting in too low a level of consumption. Thus, even when public goods can be provided by the market, there is a case for free provision to ensure the allocatively efficient level of consumption. (Those public goods such as roads which can be made excludable, for example by using toll gates, are known as *non-pure* or *quasi* public goods.)

So far in this Guide, I have stated that allocative efficiency occurs when the price charged for a good equals the marginal cost of producing the good ($P = MC$). In order to understand why **externalities** lead to market failure, I must now slightly amend my definition of allocative efficiency. True allocative efficiency occurs when the price charged for the good equals the **marginal social cost (*MSC*)** of production, and not the **marginal private cost (*MPC*)**.

If no externalities are generated in the course of production, it follows that $MSC = MPC$. This means that my earlier definition of allocative efficiency ($P = MC$) is adequate. But when there are externalities, this is no longer the case. To understand this, consider a situation in which power stations charge a price for electricity equal to the marginal *private* cost of production ($P = MPC$). The resulting outcome is only allocatively efficient if there are no externalities. If negative externalities are generated, such as pollution, and are discharged in the course of production, setting price equal to marginal *private* cost brings about an outcome in which $P < MSC$. The price charged for electricity is below the *true* marginal cost of production. As a result, the market produces too much electricity and also too much pollution. Part of the cost of producing electricity, the cost of pollution, is dumped in the atmosphere and evaded by the power station. Electricity ends up being too cheap, resulting in over-consumption and over-production. The market ends up producing the 'wrong' or allocatively inefficient quantity of electricity.

The same is true for **demerit goods** and **merit goods**, though for these goods externalities are generated in the course of *consumption* (rather than *production*). In the case of a demerit good such as tobacco, negative externalities which harm wider society can be generated when an individual smokes. In this situation, the social cost suffered by the whole community exceeds the private cost incurred by the smoker. This means that even if tobacco is consumed up to the point at which $P = MPC$, the price paid for the demerit good is less than the marginal social cost of consumption ($P < MSC$). The outcome is over-consumption and allocative inefficiency.

For a merit good such as education or healthcare, the analysis is slightly more complicated. If free market consumption leads to an outcome in which $P = MPC$, the price ends up being higher than marginal social cost ($P > MSC$). This is because the *positive* external benefit generated when a person consumes a merit good can also be modeled as a *negative* external cost. Treating the positive externality in this way, the marginal social cost of consumption turns out to be less than the marginal private cost of consumption. Even if the free market price equals the marginal private cost of consumption, it must be greater than the marginal social cost of consumption, leading to over-consumption and allocative inefficiency in a free market.

Property rights

In the 1920s, Arthur Pigou argued that the existence of externalities justified government intervention to try to correct the resulting market failures. Pigou recommended that **taxes** should be used to discourage activities that created harmful effects and **subsidies** for those creating benefits to further encourage those activities.

In contrast to the 'command and control' use of regulation, Pigovian taxes and subsidies have the advantage of working with the market by modifying market prices rather than replacing them. However, later economists (also of a free-market persuasion) argue that externalities can be better dealt with (or *internalised*) through the creation of well-defined property rights. Rights over the ownership of property are not restricted simply to an owner's rights over physical property such as buildings or land. They also include rights over resources such as clean air and water, together with intellectual property rights over the content of books and music. Property rights include control of the use of the property, the right to any benefit from the property, for example the right to breathe clean air, the right to transfer or sell the property, and the right to exclude others from the property.

If the law provides people with the property right to breathe unpolluted air, breach of this right enables victims to sue polluting companies for financial compensation. To avoid having to pay financial compensation, polluters would have to take action to eliminate the discharge of negative externalities. Alternatively, if it is impossible to eliminate a negative externality without simultaneously eliminating production of the good that produces the externality, polluters could offer people money to sign away the right to breathe unpolluted air. Either way, if the externality persists, the people who suffer pollution receive financial compensation.

Creating markets in permits to pollute

In the 1990s, another market-orientated solution started in the USA, based on a trading market in **permits** or **licences to pollute**. To begin with, maximum limits are imposed on the amount of pollution that industries are allowed to emit, followed by a steady reduction in each subsequent year (say, by 5%) of the maximum amount. But once this regulatory framework has been established, a market in traded pollution permits takes over, creating market-orientated incentives for firms to reduce pollution because they can make money out of it. Firms able to reduce pollution by more than the law requires sell their 'spare' permits to other firms, who decide not to, or cannot, reduce pollution below the maximum limit. The latter still comply with the law, even when exceeding the maximum emission limit, because they buy the spare permits sold by the former group of firms. But in the long run, even firms that find it difficult to comply with the law have an incentive to reduce pollution. By doing so, they avoid the extra costs that otherwise result from the requirement to buy pollution permits.

Government failure

There is a danger of assuming that market failure can be either reduced or completely eliminated, once identified, through appropriate government intervention: for example, by imposing taxes, controls and regulation. But there is another possibility: when the government intervenes to try to deal with a problem, far from curing or lessening the problem, intervention may make matters worse.

There are two very different approaches to the possibility of government failure, known respectively as the public interest and the public choice approach. In the **public interest** view, governments intervene benignly in the economy to eliminate waste and to achieve an efficient and socially desirable resource allocation. Markets fail and government intervention is necessary to correct market failure. Public choice theory, by contrast, argues that markets are more efficient than governments, whose intervention invariably produces an outcome inferior to that achieved by market forces. In the **public choice** view, we should be prepared to live with a degree of market failure rather than intervene in a well-intentioned but misguided way and end up creating worse problems.

Cost–benefit analysis

Cost–benefit analysis (CBA) is a technique for evaluating *all* the costs and benefits of any economic action or decision: that is, the *social* costs and benefits to the whole community and not just the *private* costs and benefits accruing to the economic agent undertaking the action. In the past, CBA has most often been used by governments to help decide whether to invest in a **major public project** such as a motorway or an airport. However, there is no reason in principle why a private sector investment, or indeed any action by a private economic agent or by the government, such as a tax change, cannot be examined by CBA.

CBA is an extension of the techniques of **investment appraisal** used by private sector firms to decide whether investment projects are commercially viable. Firms attempt to calculate all the private costs and benefits occurring in the *future* as a result of an investment or decision undertaken *now*. The central problem is guessing and putting money values to an unknown and uncertain future. But CBA is even more difficult because many of the social costs and benefits occurring in the future from an action undertaken now are externalities that are difficult to quantify. How does one put a monetary value on the saving of a human life resulting from fewer accidents on a proposed motorway? What is the social cost of the destruction of a beautiful view? It is extremely difficult to decide on all the likely costs and benefits, to draw the line on which to include and exclude, and to put monetary values on all the chosen costs and benefits accruing immediately and those that will only be received in the distant future.

Critics of CBA argue that it is pseudo-scientific — value judgements and arbitrary decisions disguised as objectivity. CBA is also criticised as a costly waste of time and money, and as a scam through which politicians distance themselves from, and induce delay in, unpopular decisions, deflecting the wrath of local communities on to supposedly impartial experts undertaking the CBA. Nevertheless, supporters of CBA argue that, for all its defects, it remains the best method of appraising public investment decisions because all the likely costs and benefits are exposed to public discussion.

Examination questions and skills

As I mentioned at the beginning of this topic, at AS the Unit 1 specification requires candidates to acquire considerable knowledge of market failure and some knowledge of government failure. The A2 Unit 3 specification for the most part then requires more advanced analysis and evaluation of the market failures covered in Unit 1. You must use the concepts of allocative efficiency and inefficiency to explain why public goods, externalities and merit and demerit goods provide examples of market failure, and you must practise analysing the causes of the various market failures, and policies such as taxation, regulation, creating markets in permits to pollute and extending property rights which aim to reduce and possibly eliminate market failures. In this Guide, DR5 is an example of a European Union context question focusing on over-fishing of fish stocks (a public good) in the North Sea.

Common examination errors

Commonly made mistakes on market failure, government failure and cost benefit analysis include the following:
- Failing to understand that market failure can be caused by both the inequitable and the inefficient functioning of markets.
- Showing a lack of awareness that monopoly and oligopoly can lead to market failure.

- Failing to apply correctly the concepts of allocative efficiency and inefficiency.
- Poorly drawn diagrams to show MPB, MSB, MPC and MSC.
- Not understanding how extending property rights might prevent market failure.
- Asserting that markets in permits to pollute are always successful.
- Wrongly asserting that government intervention always corrects market failure.
- Failing to appreciate the use and misuse of cost benefit analysis.

The labour market

These notes, which relate to AQA specification section 3.3.4, prepare you to answer AQA examination questions on:
- perfectly competitive labour markets
- imperfectly competitive or monopsonistic labour markets
- the effects of trade unions, the national minimum wage and discrimination in labour markets.

Essential information

Applying price theory to the labour market

Labour market theory is really just the price theory that you have studied in the **goods market**, but operating in the **factor market**, which is the market for the services of factors of production. Households and firms function simultaneously in both markets, but their roles are reversed. In the labour market, which is part of the factor market, firms demand labour services that households supply.

The supply of labour in a perfectly competitive labour market

The market supply curve of labour is obtained by adding together the individual supply curves of all the workers in the market. A worker's decision to supply one more hour of labour time must also mean that he or she sacrifices an hour of leisure time. For the worker to supply more labour, the hourly wage rate must rise to compensate for the fact that, as more money is earned, an extra pound means less and less, but an extra hour of leisure time sacrificed means more and more. (In economic terminology, the **marginal utility of money** falls and the **marginal utility of leisure time** rises as the worker supplies more labour, which eats into leisure time.) The resulting upward-sloping supply curve of labour is shown in Figure 18(a).

At the going hourly wage rate, a worker will not wish to supply labour beyond the point at which MU of the wage = MU of leisure, other things remaining equal. At this point, the wage received from the last hour worked yields the same utility as the last hour of leisure time enjoyed. To make it worthwhile for a worker to supply labour beyond this point, the hourly wage rate must rise: for example, from W_1 to W_2 in Figure 18(a). It is possible, however, that the supply curve may *bend backwards* above a certain wage rate (W_2 in Figure 18(b)), showing that as the wage rate rises above a critical level, the worker chooses to work fewer hours.

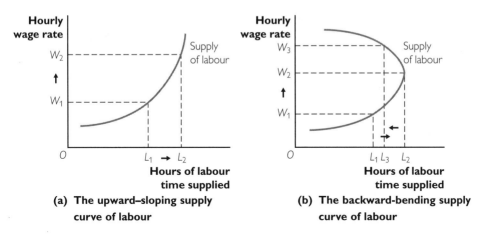

Figure 18 An individual's supply of labour

Whenever the hourly wage rate rises, an hour of leisure time becomes more expensive. Workers generally respond by working longer hours, thereby substituting more labour time in place of the now more expensive leisure time. This is the **substitution effect** of the rise in the wage rate. But an **income effect** also operates, which for some workers results in the backward-bending supply curve of labour. For most people, leisure time is a **normal good** and not an **inferior good**. A rise in the hourly wage rate increases the worker's real income, and as real income rises, so does demand for the normal good, leisure time. Above W_2 in Figure 18(b), this income effect of a wage rise becomes more powerful than the substitution effect. As a result, the worker chooses to work fewer hours so as to enjoy more leisure.

The demand for labour in a perfectly competitive labour market

Firms demand labour because they believe profit can be made by selling the goods produced by their workers. This means that the demand for labour is a **derived demand**. Just as the market supply curve of labour in a perfectly competitive labour market is the sum of the supply curves of the individual workers in the labour market, so the market demand curve for labour is the sum of the demand curves for labour of each firm in the market. Each firm's demand curve is the **marginal revenue product (MRP)** of labour curve facing the firm in the labour market.

The marginal revenue product curve shown in panel (c) of Figure 19 is obtained by multiplying the **marginal physical product (MPP)** of labour, shown in panel (a), by marginal revenue (MR), shown in panel (b). The marginal physical product or MPP of labour is just another name for the **marginal returns** (marginal product) of labour, which you first came across in the first topic, 'Firms, production and costs', pp. 17–19. Because of the law of diminishing returns, the marginal product of labour falls as additional workers are hired. As its name indicates, the MPP curve only shows the physical output produced by an extra worker — measured in whatever goods the firm produces. To convert this into a money value, the *MPP* of labour must be multiplied by marginal revenue. The end result is the *MRP* curve:

marginal physical product × marginal revenue = marginal revenue product

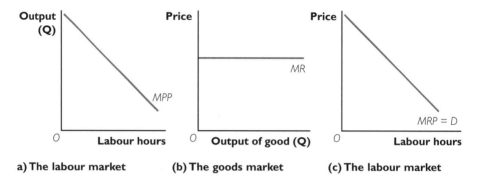

a) The labour market (b) The goods market (c) The labour market

Figure 19 Deriving a firm's demand curve for labour (the MRP curve) from the MPP curve

The equilibrium wage and level of employment in a perfectly competitive labour market

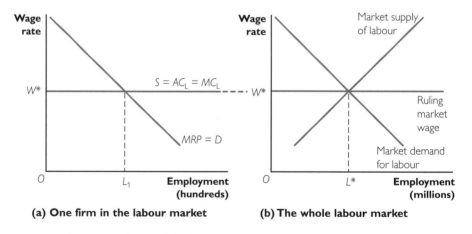

(a) One firm in the labour market (b) The whole labour market

Figure 20 The equilibrium wage rate and level of employment

Having explained the supply curves of, and the demand curves for, labour, I am now in a position to show the determination of the **equilibrium wage rate** and **level of employment**, both for a single firm or employer within the market, and also for the whole labour market. These are shown respectively in panel (a) and panel (b) of Figure 20. The equilibrium wage rate W^* and level of employment L^* are determined in panel (b), where market demand equals market supply. Panel (a) then shows each firm as a price-taker at wage rate W^*, which, as well as being the perfectly elastic supply curve of labour facing each firm, is also the **average cost of labour (AC_L)** curve and the **marginal cost of labour (MC_L)** curve. Because a firm can hire as many workers as it wants at W^*, every time an extra worker is hired, the firm's total wage bill rises by the wage paid to the new worker. Thus MC_L equals the ruling wage, which is also the AC_L (wage cost per worker).

To maximise profit when eventually selling the output produced by labour, the firm must demand labour up to the point at which:

the addition to sales revenue from employing an extra worker = the addition to production costs from employing an extra worker

or:

MRP = MC_L

In a perfectly competitive labour market, MC_L always equals the ruling wage, so the firm hires labour up to the point at which the marginal revenue product of labour equals the wage rate ($MRP = W$). This is L_1 in Figure 20(a).

Imperfectly competitive labour markets

A labour market in which there is a single employer is called a **monopsony**, and a market dominated by a single employer, but in which there are other employers, is **monopsonistic**. Monopsony means a single buyer, just as monopoly means a single seller. A monopsony is similar to a monopoly in many ways. As in monopoly, where consumers cannot choose between alternative suppliers of the good, in monopsony workers cannot choose between alternative employers. Only one firm or employer is available to hire their services. And in the same way that the market demand curve facing a monopoly supplier of a good is also the monopolist's average revenue curve, the market supply curve of labour is the monopsonist's average cost of labour (AC_L) curve. The AC_L curve shows the different wage rates that the monopsonist must pay to attract labour forces of different sizes. For example, Figure 21(a) shows a monopsony employer hiring ten workers at a daily wage or AC_L of £100 each. The diagram shows that with ten workers initially employed, the wage (or AC_L) must rise from £100 to £110 a day to attract an eleventh worker.

But in a monopsony labour market, the AC_L curve is not the marginal cost of labour (MC_L) curve. To attract extra workers, the monopsonist must raise the daily wage rate, paying the higher wage to all its workers. In this situation, the MC_L incurred by employing an extra worker includes the total amount by which the wage bill rises, and not just the wage paid to the additional worker hired. The MC_L curve is thus above the AC_L or supply curve (just as in the goods market, a monopolist's MR curve is below its AR curve). In Figure 21(a), the MC_L of employing the eleventh worker is £210 a day. This comprises the £110 paid to the eleventh worker (the darker area in

Figure 21(a)), plus the £10 extra now paid to each of the original ten workers, which totals £100 (shown by the lighter shaded area in Figure 21(a)).

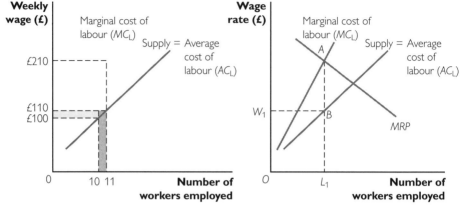

(a) AC_L and MC_L curves in monopsony

(b) **Wage and employment determination in monopsony**

Figure 21 A monopsony labour market

Figure 21(b) shows the equilibrium wage and level of employment in a monopsony labour market. As in a perfectly competitive labour market, the firm's equilibrium level of employment is determined where $MRP = MC_L$. This is at point A in Figure 21(b). However, the equilibrium wage is *below* A and *less* than the MRP of labour, being determined at point B on the supply curve of labour. Although the monopsonist *could* pay a wage determined at A and equal to the MRP of labour, without incurring a loss on the last worker employed, it has no need to. The monopsonist can employ all the workers required by paying the wage W_1, determined at point B.

Trade unions and labour markets
A trade union is an association of workers formed to protect and promote the interests of its members. A union's main function is to bargain with employers to improve wages and other conditions of work. Acting as a monopoly supplier of labour, a union may try to set the wage rate above the market-clearing wage rate, leaving employment to be determined by the amount of labour that employers hire at the wage set by the union. Figure 22(a) shows the effect of a union setting the wage rate above the market-clearing rate in a (previously) perfectly competitive labour market. Employment falls from L_1 to L_2.

But in the monopsony labour market shown in Figure 22(b), a union may be able to raise *both* the wage rate and employment. In the absence of a union, the employment level is L_1, determined at point A where $MRP = MC_L$, and the wage rate is W_1, determined at point B. If the union sets the wage rate at W_2, the kinked line W_2XS becomes the labour supply curve (and also the AC_L curve) facing the monopsonist employer. However, at wage rate W_2, the monopsonist's MC_L curve is the 'double kinked' line W_2XZV. Employment rises to L_2, the level of employment at which the MRP curve intersects the vertical section between X and Z at point C on the double-kinked MC_L curve. Both the wage rate and employment have risen compared to the situation without a union.

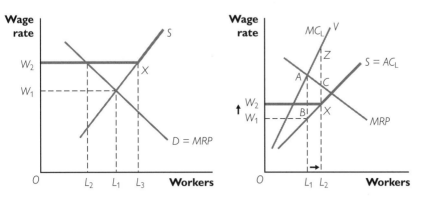

(a) **A union-set wage in a competitive labour market**

(b) **A union-set wage in a monopsony labour market**

Figure 22 The effect of introducing a trade union into competitive and monopsony labour markets

The effect of a national minimum wage

Figure 22 can also be used to explain and analyse the possible effects of introducing a national minimum wage rate. In a competitive labour market, a minimum wage rate set at W_2 increases wages for the workers who keep their jobs, but creates unemployment. By contrast, both wages *and* employment may rise if the labour market is monopsonistic.

The theory of wage discrimination

Just as *price discrimination* occurs when firms with *monopoly* power charge different prices based on customers' different willingness to pay, so wage discrimination takes place when employers with *monopsony* power pay different wage rates based on

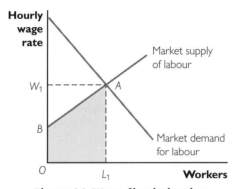

Figure 23 Wage discrimination

workers' different willingness to supply labour. In the absence of wage discrimination, all workers in a competitive labour market (shown in Figure 23) receive a wage rate of W_1, determined by supply and demand. Employers' total wage costs are shown by the rectangle bounded by points OW_1AL_1. But if, instead of paying W_1 to *all* workers, employers pay *each* worker the minimum they are prepared to work for, the total wage bill falls to equal the shaded 'wedge' area bounded by the points $OBAL_1$. Employers thus gain at the expense of workers, which is why firms pay, and trade unions resist, discriminatory wages whenever possible.

Other explanations of different wages

Even in highly competitive labour markets, wage differences exist, largely because the labour demand and supply curves are in different positions in different labour markets, reflecting factors such as varying labour productivity, ability and required skill. Also, different jobs have different non-monetary characteristics, often in the form of job satisfaction or dissatisfaction. Other things being equal, a worker must be paid a higher wage to compensate for any relative unpleasantness in the job. An **equalising wage differential** is the payment that must be made to compensate a worker for the different non-monetary characteristics of jobs so that, following the payment, the worker has no incentive to switch between jobs or labour markets.

Different wages paid to different groups of workers may also result from forms of **labour market discrimination** unrelated to the theory of wage discrimination. Some employers discriminate on the basis of race, religion, gender and age, even though such discrimination is usually illegal. Workers suffering labour market discrimination have poorer job opportunities and are generally less well paid than workers fortunate enough to avoid such discrimination.

Examination questions and skills

Essay questions in the examination are likely to ask for explanation, analysis and evaluation of the functioning of different labour markets (perfectly competitive and/or monopsonistic), whereas context data-response questions might home in on particular real-world labour markets and require the application of the theoretical concepts explained in these notes to the issues posed by the question. Data-response Question 6 on labour migration between the UK and other EU countries centres on how different wage rates and labour market conditions affect the international mobility of labour.

Common examination errors

Commonly made mistakes on the labour market include the following:
- Failing to understand the reversal of roles of households and firms in the labour market, with firms exercising demand for labour and households exercising supply.
- Failing to appreciate that maximising principles (profit for firms and utility for workers) underlie labour market theory.

- Writing about the whole market when the question asks for analysis of one firm within the market, and vice versa.
- Inaccurate analysis of the demand for labour in terms of marginal productivity theory.
- Lack of understanding of monopsonistic labour markets.
- Writing 'commonsense' superficial accounts of wage differences without using labour market theory.

Income, wealth and poverty

These notes, which relate to AQA specification sections 3.3.4 and 3.3.5, prepare you to answer AQA examination questions on:
- the distribution of income and wealth
- notions of equity
- the problem of poverty
- government policies to alleviate poverty and influence the distribution of income and wealth

Essential information

Income and wealth

Income and wealth illustrate the key difference between flow and stock concepts in economics. Income is a **flow**, measured per period of time: for example, weekly, monthly or annually. The **stock** of wealth, by contrast, accumulates over time. The different **factors of production** receive different types of income. Employees are paid wages and salaries; owners of land and property receive rent; interest is paid to lenders of financial capital; and profit is the residual earned by the owners of businesses and entrepreneurs. Transfers, such as unemployment benefits, are another very important type of income, especially for the poor. As the name indicates, transfers shift income from taxpayers to benefit recipients, without production of a good or service by the person receiving the benefit.

People can hold wealth in **physical assets** such as land, houses, art and antiques, or in **financial assets** such as stocks and shares. Houses and shares are forms of **marketable wealth**, whose value can appreciate (go up in value) or depreciate (go down in value). Some forms of wealth are **non-marketable**: for example, the stock of wealth accumulated when a person contributes to a pension scheme cannot be sold to someone else.

Inequalities in the distribution of income and wealth

In the UK, as in most other countries, the distributions of income and wealth are both unequal, but the distribution of wealth is significantly more unequal than the distribution of income. The link between wealth and income partly explains this. For the better-off, wealth generates investment income, part of which — being saved — then adds to wealth and generates even more income. The poor, by contrast, who possess little or no wealth, also have incomes (from low-paid jobs and/or welfare benefits) that are too low to allow saving and the accumulation of wealth. The tax system also provides an explanation. In the UK income is usually taxed, but wealth is generally untaxed (except through **inheritance tax** and **capital gains tax** which are easily avoidable).

When describing and explaining the distribution of income, it is useful to understand the difference between a number of different measures of income: original income, gross income, disposable income, post-tax income and final income. The relationship between these different measures of income is shown in Figure 24.

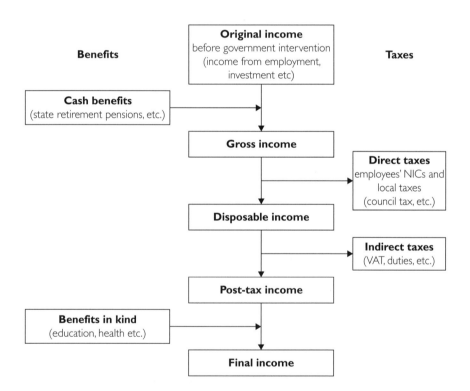

Figure 24 The different ways in which income is measured and their relation to taxes and benefits

The measurement of inequalities in the distribution of income

The extent to which the distribution of income is equal or unequal can be illustrated on **Lorenz curve** diagrams, such as that drawn in Figure 25, with the degree of inequality measured by a statistic known as a **Gini coefficient**.

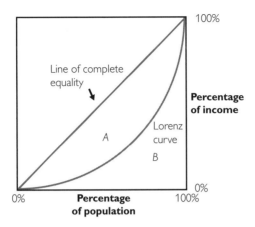

Figure 25 The Lorenz curve

The Lorenz curve in Figure 25 shows population on the horizontal axis, measured in cumulative percentages from 0 to 100%. The vertical axis shows the cumulative percentage of income received by the population. If incomes were distributed equally, the Lorenz curve would lie along the diagonal line. The nearer the Lorenz curve is to the diagonal, the more equal is the distribution of income. The Gini coefficient measures the area between the Lorenz curve and the diagonal as a ratio of the total area under the diagonal.

In Figure 25 the Gini coefficient is calculated using the following formula:

$$\text{Gini coefficient} = \frac{\text{area } A}{\text{area } A + \text{area } B}$$

Reasons for an unequal distribution of income

The labour market theory covered in the previous topic, 'The labour market' (pp. 52–59), provides part of the explanation for income inequalities. Different supply and demand conditions (including differing labour productivity) in different labour markets lead to different equilibrium wages, while employers' monopsony power and an absence of countervailing union power might drive down wages in particular labour markets. However, the lowest incomes are received by the unwaged rather than by the low-waged. The unemployed and elderly people who are solely reliant on the state old age pension are two of the groups with the lowest incomes.

In part, the growing *relative* inequality of the unemployed and the elderly has been caused by the way welfare benefits are adjusted each year. Before the early 1980s, unemployment benefit, the state pension and other welfare benefits increased each year in line with changes in the **index of average earnings**, so the unwaged shared in increasing national prosperity. As average earnings generally rise faster than inflation, the real income of benefit recipients increased by the same amount as the average of people in work. But since the early 1980s, welfare benefits have been index linked to the retail price index (RPI), which generally rises by less than the index of average earnings. As a result, inequality between people with jobs and those without jobs grew. In 2006, the Labour government announced its intention to restore the index linking between pensions and earnings 'sometime after 2012'. However, the impact of the 2008 recession, a rapidly ageing population and the likelihood of the Labour government being voted out of office in 2010, have probably put paid to this worthy intention.

Inequality, market failure and government failure

Unregulated market forces tend to produce highly unequal distributions of income and wealth, which many economists deem inequitable, unjust or unfair. They argue that government intervention, usually through **progressive taxation** (taxing the rich more proportionately than the poor) and **transfers** from rich to poor, should be used to reduce inequalities. But free-market economists counter by arguing that such intervention, although well intentioned, results in problems of government failure that are worse than the supposed market failure that intervention aims to correct. They argue that, if taxes are too progressive and benefits too generous, labour market incentives are destroyed. The economy becomes less competitive, economic growth stalls, and the poor end up being *absolutely* worse off than they would have been had growth been faster, even though *relative* to the rich, the poor are better off. The poor would benefit more, they argue, from greater inequality, faster growth and the **trickle down effect** that might occur as the rich spend their wealth and high incomes on goods and services produced by the poor.

So what has actually happened in the UK? During much of the twentieth century, progressive taxation and transfers reduced income inequalities, except during the 1980s and 1990s when free-market supply-side policies widened inequalities. At the beginning of the twenty-first century, government policy had some success in reducing income inequality, but as I briefly mentioned earlier, inequalities have recently been widening once again.

Horizontal and vertical equity

Equity, which means fairness or justness, is a **normative** concept (a matter of opinion), whereas the closely related, but not identical, concept of equality can be measured and is therefore a **positive** concept. Government intervention in the economy, which treats people *in the same circumstances* equally, obeys the principle of horizontal equity. For example, horizontal equity occurs when households with the same income and personal circumstances (for example, the same number of children) pay the same income tax and are eligible for the same welfare benefits.

Vertical equity is much more controversial, since it justifies taking income from the rich (on the grounds that they do not need it) and redistributing their income to the poor (on the grounds that they do need it). The distribution of income after taxation and receipt of transfers is judged more equitable. Achieving greater vertical equity can conflict with another principle of intervention, the **benefit principle**, which argues that those who receive most benefit from government spending (such as motorists benefiting from roads) should pay the most in taxes.

Poverty

Poverty is closely related to inequalities in the distribution of income and wealth. However, we must distinguish between *absolute* poverty and *relative* poverty. Because the UK is a high-income developed economy, in which welfare benefits provide a minimum income and safety net for most of the poor, very few people are absolutely poor. For the most part, the problem of poverty in the UK is one of relative poverty. A household is in **relative poverty** if its income is below a specified proportion of average income for all households: for example, less than a third of average income. Possible causes of relative poverty include: unemployment, especially long-term unemployment; old age and longevity; single parenthood; the decline of employment opportunities in traditional industries and skill fields; lack of education and training; the fall in the value of welfare and unemployment benefits relative to wages and salaries; and the higher incomes and tax cuts enjoyed by the better-off.

By contrast, **absolute poverty** occurs when income is below a particular specified level. When *all* incomes grow, *absolute* poverty falls, but *relative* poverty falls only if low incomes grow at a faster rate than average incomes.

Government policies to reduce poverty

By reducing inequalities in the distribution of income, progressive taxation and transfers (welfare benefits) can reduce absolute and relative poverty — providing labour market incentives, competitiveness and economic growth do not worsen significantly. All economists agree, however, that *absolute* poverty, though not necessarily *relative* poverty, can best be reduced by fast and sustained economic growth and by creating jobs. Very low incomes generally result from being *unwaged* through unemployment or old age, rather than *low-waged* and in employment.

The poverty trap or earnings trap

In so far as low-waged workers are poor, their ability to escape from poverty may be limited by the existence of the poverty trap (or earnings trap). The immediate cause of the poverty trap is the overlap — which is illustrated in Figure 26 — between the income tax threshold (the level of income at which income tax starts to be paid) and the means-tested welfare benefits ceiling (the level of income at which means-tested transfer incomes cease to be paid). When welfare benefits are means-tested, a person's right to claim the benefit is reduced and eventually disappears completely, as income rises. A low-paid worker caught within this zone of overlap not only pays income tax and national insurance contributions (NICs) on each extra pound earned; they also lose part or all of the right to claim benefits. Thus low-paid workers and their families whose income falls within this zone of overlap become trapped in relative poverty, since any increase in their pay results in little or no increase — and in extreme cases, in a fall — in their disposable income. The effective **marginal rate of taxation** of workers in poorly paid occupations is therefore very high indeed when the loss of means-tested benefits is added to deductions through income tax and NICs.

The poverty trap could be eliminated by getting rid of the zone of overlap in the **income pyramid** illustrated in Figure 26. The income tax threshold could be raised to take low-waged households out of the tax net. Means-tested benefits could be replaced by **universal benefits** (benefits claimable as of right, and unrelated to income). But as taxes would have to increase to pay for any substantial increase in universal benefits, the poor might end up more heavily taxed. By preventing employers paying 'poverty wages', the **national minimum wage** also reduces both poverty and the poverty trap, though this is counterproductive if the minimum wage increases unemployment.

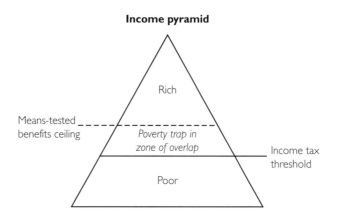

Figure 26 The poverty trap

Examination questions and skills

Examination questions are likely to ask for description of inequalities in the distributions of income and/or wealth, explanation and analysis of the causes of identified inequalities, assessment of the implications of inequality for the UK economy and/or evaluation of policies that governments use or might use to reduce inequality. EQ3 assesses your knowledge of the meaning and causes of poverty, and then asks for an evaluation of government policies that aim to reduce poverty.

Common examination errors

Commonly made mistakes on income, wealth and poverty include the following:
- Confusing income as a *flow* with wealth as a *stock*.
- Inability to explain and analyse inequalities and poverty in terms of market failure and government failure.
- Confusing equity with equality.
- Lack of understanding of how progressive taxes and transfers can, in principle, reduce inequality.
- Failing to apply supply and demand analysis and labour market theory to explain income inequality.

- Confusing absolute poverty and relative poverty.
- Lack of awareness of poverty traps other than the earnings trap: for example, to get a job a person may need a home, but to get a home a person may need a job.

Questions
&
Answers

This section includes nine examination-style questions designed to be a key learning, revision and exam preparation resource. There are six data-response questions (DRQs) and three essay questions (EQs). The six DRQs are similar in layout, structure and style to the questions in Section A of the Unit 3 examination. Questions 1, 2 and 3 are set on The global context, and Questions 4, 5 and 6 are set on The European Union context. For all the data-response questions, the word *context* provides a scenario for analysing the impact of some event or events occurring in the wider world or in the European Union upon an aspect of the UK microeconomy, typically UK businesses or industries.

The three essay questions (EQs) included in this book are similar to the three questions from which you must choose one in Section B of the Unit 3 examination. Important specification topics such as the theory of the firm, labour markets, market failure, cost–benefit analysis and poverty perhaps lend themselves more to essay questions than to 'context' data-response questions. However, most if not all questions, be they data response or essay questions, are likely to be of an *applied* nature, requiring application of knowledge and theory to analyse and evaluate real world issues and problems.

This section also includes:

- A student's answer varying from grade A* to grade D standard for each DRQ and EQ.
- Examiner's comments on each student's answer, explaining — where relevant — how the answer could be improved and a higher grade or mark achieved. These comments are denoted by the symbol e.

Note: It is important to understand the difference between two types of marks that GCE examining boards award for candidates' work: **raw marks** and marks awarded according to the **Uniform Mark Scale (UMS)**.

Raw marks are the marks awarded out of 40 (for each DRQ and EQ) by the examiner who reads your script. After all, the grade boundaries have been set as raw marks, each candidate's raw mark for the Unit 3 paper is converted into a UMS mark. UMS marks have the same grade boundaries — for all subjects and all unit exams. These are: grade A* 90%; grade A: 80%; grade B: 70%; grade C: 60%; grade D: 50%; grade E: 40%. In economics, a raw mark of around 75% for both A2 Unit exams should achieve the UMS of 90% required for an A* grade, providing a sufficiently high AS mark has already been earned.

The marks awarded for students' answers to each DRQ and EQ in the following pages are raw marks and not UMS marks. A likely grade is indicated at the end of each student's answer, based on the qualities shown in each part of the answer. I have used the grade boundaries: A*: 75%; A: 65%; B: 57%; C: 50%; and D: 43%. The boundary mark for grade E (which I haven't used) is 36%. The actual raw mark at which a particular grade boundary is set varies from examination to examination.

d ata-response question

1

Data-response questions
The global context

Question 1 The global oil market and UK firms

Total for this question: 40 marks

Study **Extracts A, B** and **C**, and answer **all** parts of the question which follow.

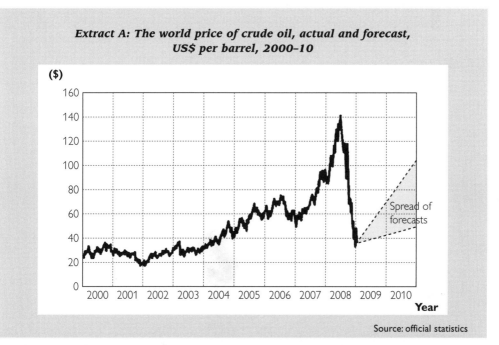

*Extract A: The world price of crude oil, actual and forecast,
US$ per barrel, 2000–10*

Source: official statistics

Extract B: The changing world price of crude oil

On 29 May 2009, the price of crude oil rose to $66 a barrel, well above the $32.7 low 1
to which the price had fallen in February 2009. Despite recession dampening world
demand for oil, the price rise was a response to upbeat comments made earlier in the
week at an OPEC meeting in Vienna about rising oil demand in Asia. OPEC also
warned that speculative investment was partly to blame for the increase in prices. 5
'Speculators are coming back, not only to oil, but to all commodities. We are not
happy.'

data-response question

At its Vienna meeting, OPEC agreed to leave its production level unchanged at 24.8m barrels a day, betting that the strengthening of the global economy would cause oil prices to rise. Previously, OPEC had announced three big output cuts, as the cartel tried to prevent the price from falling. However, OPEC members only delivered 80 per cent of these promised cuts. 10

Adam Sieminski, chief energy economist at Deutsche Bank, said that the 'rise in the oil market sentiment and oil bullishness seems to us based more on hope than fact. The rise has occurred in spite of fairly bearish fundamentals, with poor demand, high 15 supply, brimming inventories, and plenty of spare capacity.' However, oil prices — and speculative investment flows — were well below 2008's peak, when oil traded at almost $150 a barrel.

Adapted from news sources

Extract C: How changes in the output and price of oil may affect UK industries

On 29th October 2008 at the London Stock Exchange, eight leading UK companies 1 launched a report, *The Oil Crunch: Securing the UK's energy future*, warning that peak production of cheap, easily available oil is likely to occur by 2013, posing a grave risk to UK firms.

The availability and price of oil affect almost every aspect of our economy and our 5 day-to-day lives: the way we travel, where we work, what we eat, how we power our homes and buildings; and how we manufacture goods here in the UK. The 'easy oil' that makes up most of the existing capacity is declining fast, and the new capacity coming on stream — often from 'not-so-easy oil' — will not replace it fast enough from 2011 onwards. 10

Agriculture and manufacturing are the two sectors of the UK economy that will be most affected by the move to 'not-so-easy' oil. Modern food production is oil dependent across the entire value chain from the field to the delivered package — and the whole manufacturing industry is heavily energy-dependent. In the near future, we'll cycle and walk more, use lots of public transport, reduce our long-haul 15 holidays and our transport will be fuelled by sustainable bio-liquids and electricity. Car companies increasingly are betting on electricity as the fuel of the future, though Britain lags behind other countries in investment in recharging stations.

The electric vehicle's limited range is frequently cited as being a barrier to widespread uptake and to a certain extent it is. The electric cars appearing on the 20 market today have ranges of between 70 and 110 miles. Cars capable of greater ranges before recharging are not far from being a reality as more and more manufacturers enter the market. Many of the major vehicle manufacturers will be releasing electric models into their product range by 2010, hence electric vehicles are edging closer to mainstream acceptability. It is worth bearing in mind that 99% of all ²⁵ passenger car journeys are of 100 miles or less. Electric car technology is therefore close to being sufficiently mature to account for the vast majority of journeys driven in the UK.

Adapted from news sources

(1) **With the help of Extract A, identify two significant features of the changes in the world price of crude oil over the period from 2000 to 2010.** (5 marks)

(2) **Extract B (lines 15–16) mentions how 'brimming inventories, and plenty of spare capacity' might affect the price of oil. Analyse how both these factors might influence the price of crude oil.** (10 marks)

(3) **Using the data and your economic knowledge, discuss how future changes in the price of crude oil may affect UK firms involved in economic activities such as manufacturing, agriculture or transport.** (25 marks)

■ ■ ■

Candidate's answer

(1) For most of the period shown for actual measurement (2000–08), the price of oil rose steadily (apart from relatively small seasonal fluctuations and one longer more pronounced dip in late 2006/early 2007), from approximately US$22 a barrel at the beginning of 2000 to peak at over $140 a barrel in mid-2008. However, for the last 6 months of 2008, the price fell rapidly from the peak of $140 a barrel to less than $40 a barrel at the end of the period of actual measurement in December 2008. **5/5 marks**

> 🖉 Part (1) of the Unit 3 (and 4) data-response questions are no more difficult than the similar questions set in the Units 1 and 2 AS examinations. Given the wording of the question, all you have to do to earn full marks is to identify and briefly describe two points of comparison, and to back up each point with evidence drawn from the data and provided by the statistics in the data. The candidate has done this, so earns all 5 marks.

(2) 'Brimming inventories' refers to stocks of crude oil already extracted from the earth's crust, presumably stored in tanks, oil tankers, or underground. 'Spare capacity' probably refers to oil refining capacity and transport capacity, i.e. idle oil tankers, that are not currently being used. Taken together, they mean that a sudden increase in worldwide demand for oil could quickly be met by increasing the supply of crude oil onto the market. As a result the price of oil should not rise by very much, or might not rise at all. **5/10 marks**

data-response question

 Mark schemes for part (2) questions usually start by indicating that marks are available for accurate definitions of concepts or terms in the question. So get into the habit of reading the question carefully and then providing *short* definitions of any terms in the question. The candidate does this, so earns 2 marks out of the 10 available. (Check mark schemes to see how many marks are usually available for definitions.) Unfortunately, however, the answer does not develop and fully *analyse* the reasons briefly stated for the likely effect of 'brimming inventories' and 'spare capacity' on the price of crude oil. Remember, the Unit 3 (and Unit 4) exams are synoptic, testing AS material. This question invites application of basic supply and demand analysis. The candidate *mentions* the effect of brimming inventories and spare capacity on supply, but does not develop the analysis. Consequently, only 3 marks are picked up for the use of theory. Besides developing relevant theory, a very good answer might have argued that, since Extract B states that the price of oil was increasing *despite* brimming inventories and 'spare capacity', demand factors, such as the effect of speculation on demand, overrode the supply factors. However, full marks can be earned without this observation.

(3) All three of the economic activities mentioned in the question (manufacturing, agriculture and transport) are currently highly-dependent on oil as the main source of the large amount of energy used in the course of production. Along with raw materials such as steel in the car industry, energy is one of the main inputs or factors of production used to produce final output. Without the required inputs, output cannot be produced. When 'oil crises' occurred in relatively recent history, with the oil tap suddenly being turned off, large parts of manufacturing had to restrict output, and transport was greatly curtailed, at least for a few weeks.

However, the question mentions the price of oil rather than the quantity of oil. Of course the two are closely related. Extract B mentions how OPEC, the oil producers' cartel, sometimes deliberately restricts output in order to force the price up. In this situation, at least in the short term, UK businesses are affected more by the immediate shortage of oil rather than by its increasing price.

Extract C focuses by contrast on the much more long term likely effect on the price of oil resulting from depletion of global oil stocks. As my diagram below shows, the global supply curve of oil is likely to shift to the left, partly because 'peak production' has been past, and partly because more and more of the oil extracted from the earth's surface is 'not so easy' oil with high production costs, rather than 'easy oil' with low production costs. My diagram also shows the global demand curve shifting to the right as more and more 'emerging market' countries such as China and India industrialise and become richer. A growing percent of Chinese and Indian citizens now own cars, which currently are fueled by oil. As a result of the combined shifts, the world price of oil to rises from P_1 to P_2.

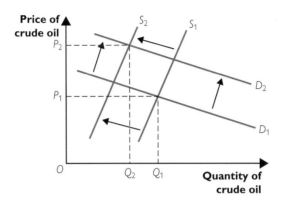

So what will be the effect on UK economic activities? Manufacturing has fallen significantly in importance in the UK and much of the shrunken manufacturing sector uses much less oil than previously. Service sector industries such as finance use less oil than manufacturing. Oil is, of course, still the main fuel used in transport, with the closely related product of natural gas being used for heating and for the production of electricity. The prices of both these sources of fuel have increased rapidly in recent years, and for the reasons I explained earlier, will continue to rise. If UK firms remain dependent on oil and gas, their costs of production will rise, and they will be vulnerable to sudden supply shortages. They may become even more uncompetitive in world markets. Bankruptcies and permanent recession may loom. The issue, therefore, is whether or not UK firms can become less dependent on oil and gas, largely through the development of substitute sources of energy. It has been suggested, for example, that only airlines should use biofuel, electric-powered cars should replace oil-driven cars as quickly as possible, and that more and more electricity should be generated from wind and nuclear power. Extract C is fairly optimistic, arguing that electric-powered cars will soon be a realistic alternative to the use of the internal combustion engine.

The eventual effect of rising oil prices on UK firms therefore depends on a number of factors, and we can only speculate on the likely effect of each factor. Much will depend on the ability of different industries to adapt to new technologies and the speed at which they can do so. Changes in relative prices will provide incentives for firms to adapt and change. However, the overall state of the British (and the global) economy is also important. On the one hand new technologies, created as firms are forced to adapt to higher oil prices and oil shortages, usher in a new era of continued economic growth. But on the other hand, changes in world markets for oil and natural gas may lead to economic stagnation, world conflicts and protectionism in which the UK economy suffers, and GDP and standards of living fall. In such a depressed economic environment, unless they were sufficiently competitive, British firms would probably perform badly. **25/25 marks**

data-response question

e It is impossible in the stresses and strains of an examination, and given the time available (roughly 1 hour for the data question), to write a perfect answer covering all the possible issues and arguments. To earn a mark in the highest mark band (Level 5: 22 to 25 marks), the answer has to provide, not perfection, but good analysis and good evaluation. This is what the candidate has done, so the answer earns full marks. If the candidate had made no reference to the data or to UK economic activities, Level 5 would not have been reached. However, in this answer, there is sufficient reference to the data and to UK firms for these hurdles in the mark scheme to have been passed. Note that the words *manufacturing*, *agriculture* and *transport* in the question provide prompts. The accompanying words 'such as' mean that answers do not have to cover all or any of these economic activities. An answer could focus on other activities such as electricity generation or fishing, though such an approach would be unlikely.

Scored 35/40   88% = grade A*

ata-response question

Question 2 The effect of the collapse of General Motors on the UK car industry

Total for this question: 40 marks

Study **Extracts A**, **B and C**, and then answer **all** parts of the question which follow.

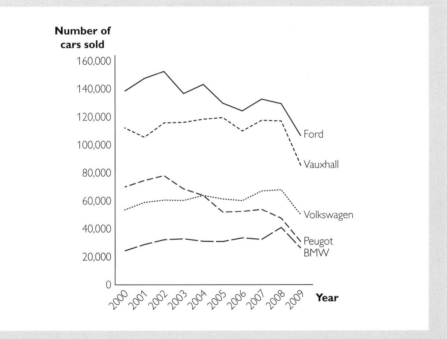

Extract A: Sales of the five leading UK car brands, 2000–09

Source: motor industry statistics

Extract B: General Motors and economies of scale in car production

For much of the twentieth century, leading car manufacturers believed that 'big is 1 always better'. According to this view, large size means that the advantages of mass production, economies of scale and assembly line production can be benefited from to the full. Based on this business model, General Motors, whose principal factories were located in Detroit, USA, became the world's largest car company. At its height, 5 GM's output had a value exceeding the GDP of many of the world's nations.

data-response question

By 1980, General Motors was manufacturing 'world cars' in factories located in a number of countries, assembling the cars from parts and components manufactured in other GM factories scattered throughout the world. As the map below shows, by 1980, GM's European plants, badged under the Opel and Vauxhall brand names, 10 assembled finished cars from components shipped from GM factories located thousands of miles away.

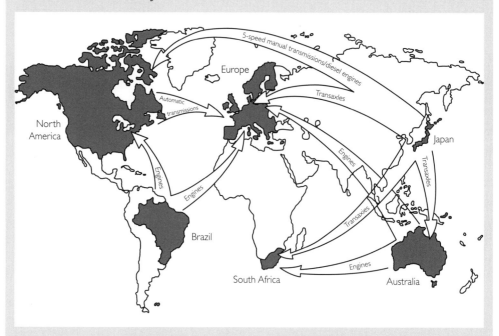

Putting General Motors' world car together

But by 2009, GM had lost touch with what consumers wanted. The company was still producing badly designed gas-guzzling 4 by 4s, sports utility vehicles (SUVs) and Hummers, at a time when most of the world's consumers were demanding 15 energy-efficient smaller vehicles embodying cutting-edge technology.

Adapted from news sources

Extract C: Crisis at Vauxhall Motors

In June 2009, General Motors was declared bankrupt. To raise money to pay for GM's 1 revival as a new company, supported and partly owned by the American government, GM's overseas assets were sold. GM's main European subsidiary, GM Europe, was sold to new owners. In 2009, GM traded under the Opel brand name in continental Europe, and as the Vauxhall brand in the UK market. 5

Intense competition from Asian car producers, together with the effects of recession and overcapacity, meant that factory closures were viewed as inevitable in traditional car-producing countries. For GM Europe, the question was: would closures be in Germany, in other EU countries such as Belgium and Spain, or at the company's Vauxhall plants in the UK? 10

Before the sell-off, GM Europe was a truly European automobile company. However, company headquarters, product design, the four main factories and 25,000 employees were located in Germany rather than in the UK. GM Europe's UK factories at Luton and on the Merseyside were much smaller than its German factories. Over the years the British plants had become mere branch factories, employing a total of 15 5,000 workers. Nevertheless in 2009, Vauxhall was one of the UK's leading car brands, second only to Ford, and accounting for 14% of all UK car sales. Vauxhall's Corsa, Astra, Insignia and Zafira brands were four of the top-selling models in the UK market. For GM, the UK was the largest market in Europe, ahead of Russia and Germany. 20

When the sell-off became inevitable, the German government quickly provided large-scale funds to try to secure the future of all Opel's German manufacturing plants and to protect German jobs. Although this was in Germany's interest, such financial support broke EU law relating to EU competition policy and the rules of the Single European market. By guaranteeing German jobs and plants, it was widely 25 believed that the German government's policy would lead to the closure of GM Europe's factories elsewhere in Europe, especially in the UK. It appeared that Vauxhall was about to suffer the negative consequences of being a bit-part player in a sprawling multinational business.

Source: News Reports, 2000

(1) Using Extract A, compare the changes in the sales of Vauxhall cars with those of Ford cars in the UK market over the years from April 2001 to March 2009. (5 marks)

(2) '…large size means that the advantages of mass production, economies of scale and assembly line production can be benefited from to the full.' (Extract B, lines 2–4). Analyse how these methods of production can benefit large firms in the car industry. (10 marks)

(3) 'Intense competition from Asian car producers, together with the effects of recession and overcapacity, mean that factory closures are inevitable in traditional car-producing countries. (Extract C, lines 6–8). Using the data and your economic knowledge, discuss whether the UK government should intervene to prevent the closure of British factories in manufacturing industries such as the car industry. (25 marks)

■ ■ ■

data-response question

Candidate's answer

(1) Sales of Ford cars exceeded those of Vauxhall throughout the period shown by the data. This was because Ford cars are superior to Vauxhall cars and are better advertised. Sales of both Ford and Vauxhall cars exceed those of VW, Peugeot and BMW. **1/5 marks**

> *e* This answer exhibits four commonly occurring reasons why candidates fail to earn many marks for the first part of a data-response question. First, the candidate makes only one *relevant* point of comparison, while more than one is required. Check mark schemes for past exam papers to see how many of the 5 available marks are awarded for a point of comparison. This will tell you how many points of comparison need to be made. Obviously, if a question states that only two points of comparison are required, simply obey the question. This answer includes a second point of comparison, but since it is not one asked for by the question, it earns no marks. Second, the candidate provides no statistical backup, and third the answer drifts away from comparison into trying (badly) to explain why more Ford cars are sold than Vauxhall cars. Part (1) data-response questions *never* ask for explanation or discussion of causes.

(2) These methods of production benefit large firms by contributing to lower costs of production. This is illustrated on my diagram below, which shows a firm benefiting from economies of scale as it increases the level of output, before suffering from diseconomies of scale beyond the level of output Q_2.

The methods of production also enable firms to make larger profits. Profit is the difference between total revenue and total cost. As my diagram shows, falling average costs (economies of scale), increase a typical firm's supernormal profit, shown by the shaded area on my diagram.

Not all car firms benefit from mass production, economies of scale and assembly line production. Car firms such as Morgan, Rolls Royce and Bentley produce only a small number of cars each year and benefit from economies of small-scale production. **2/10 marks**

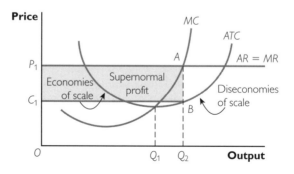

e This is a thoroughly confused answer, typical of those written by candidates who don't understand the theory of the firm, and in particular, the difference between short-run and long-run costs of production. The answer misses the opportunity at the outset by failing to define any of the concepts in the question. Of the three methods of production stated in the question, only economies of scale are mentioned in the specification. At the very least, this concept should have been accurately defined, together possibly either with costs or average costs of production. Economies of scale are falling *long-run* average costs of production. The answer does mention costs of production, but by not showing an understanding of *average* costs of production, it is much too vague. The diagram is also a mess, wrongly illustrating economies and diseconomies of scale on a short-run cost curve for a perfectly competitive firm. Economies of scale (and their opposite diseconomies of scale) are long-run concepts. They cannot be shown on a short-run cost curve. Also, the context of the question does not indicate a large number of small firms competing against each other. A diagram showing a perfectly competitive firm is completely inappropriate for this answer. Nevertheless, 2 marks have been awarded, for stating that economies of scale enable firms to make larger profits, and for a brief but not very relevant mention of car firms.

(3) For much of the twentieth century, the car industry was one of the main industries in the UK, and in other developed industrialised countries such as the USA, Germany, France and Italy. The automobile industry is, of course, a manufacturing industry, and also until quite recently, manufacturing was more important than services in the UK. The car industry was important, not only for its direct contribution to UK GDP, employment and trade, but because of the demand it created for components supplied by a large number of generally smaller component manufacturers such as firms that make windscreens, tyres, gear boxes and engines.

However in the second half of the twentieth century, UK car manufacturers began to experience competition, first from other European car firms, then from Japan, and more recently from Korea. In the future, even more intense competition may come from China and India. At the same time, UK-owned car manufacturers such as Rover were bought up by overseas car companies. Ford and Vauxhall motors had always been American-owned. The Japanese car companies, Toyota, Nissan and Honda also invested from scratch in brand-new British factories, producing cars for export to other EU countries as well as for UK customers.

The UK car industry is still one of Britain's biggest industries and currency earners through its export sales, but car imports now exceed exports. Britain has a balance of trade deficit in cars. But there is now world-wide overproduction of cars, exacerbated by the decline in demand in recessionary conditions. Simple arithmetic tells us that some car factories will have to close;

data-response question

the question is where. The case for allowing the closure of British car plants is that Britain's comparative and competitive advantage has moved away from manufacturing and into services, particularly financial services. We should respond to the laws of markets and allow the winding down of industries in which we no longer have a comparative advantage (lower opportunity cost in production).

The case against this argument is that as the 2008 recession shows, financial services cannot be relied upon. Arguably, in the boom years of the early 2000s, the UK economy became over-dependent on financial services and vulnerable to dire consequences if financial services suddenly collapsed (as they did). There is a case for having a diversified economy, with manufacturing as one of its core elements. And services need something to service. Without successful manufacturing industries, there may be little to service. Britain needs industries that employ manual workers. Over-reliance on services may mean that much of the working population will end up being employed in low-skilled service jobs, or simply unemployed.

I shall conclude by bringing in the concepts of market failure and government failure. Market forces are taking car manufacturing to other countries, particularly in Asia. This can be viewed as the natural functioning of markets, rather than as market failure. If the UK government intervenes to try to correct a wrongly-perceived market failure, it may cost UK taxpayers a huge amount of wasted money. The government may end up propping up 'losers' rather than picking 'winners'. If this is the case, government failure will result. But on the other hand, car manufacturing may be moving to Asia, not solely because of lower wage costs and a more willing, pliable work force in developing and newly-industrialising countries, but because the car industries in such countries are already being propped up by government subsidies and protectionism. To create a level playing field, there is a case for similar subsidy and protectionism in the UK. Extract C in the question suggests that in the case of Opel and Vauxhall, the German government is providing money to save Opel at the expense of Vauxhall. If this has happened, there may also be a case for the UK government intervening to try to protect output, exports and jobs in the British car industry. **19/25 marks**

🖉 The answer to the final part of the question saves the candidate and allows a respectable, though not a high, overall grade to be earned. The candidate's answer to part (2) had shown a weak understanding of microeconomic theory at A2. Fortunately for part (3), the candidate wrote a good overview answer that was strong on economic history, without including much microeconomics, apart from some application of the concepts of market failure and government failure. Knowledge of economic history extending more than the 10 years before the exam is not required, though some earlier knowledge of UK economic cycles may be needed. In this case, the economic history provides a sound foundation for the later parts of the answer, but in itself it does not earn marks. However, the A2 exams are synoptic, which means it is permissible to introduce and apply relevant macroeconomic arguments. In this case, the candidate succinctly applied the concepts of changing comparative and competitive advantage, without getting bogged down in unnecessary detail. It is actually quite difficult to place this answer in the appropriate level in the mark scheme. Level 3 requires an 'adequate answer with some correct analysis but limited evaluation'. I think the answer is rather better than this, so I have placed it in mid-Level 4 (17–21 marks: 'Good analysis but limited evaluation'). Some of the evaluation is quite good, but I don't think that the analysis and evaluation taken together are sufficiently strong for the answer to reach Level 5: 'Good analysis and evaluation'.

Scored 22/40   55% = mid-grade C

ata-response question

Question 3   Global competition and the UK call centre industry

Total for this question: 40 marks

Study **Extracts A**, **B**, **C** and **D**, and then answer **all** parts of the question which follow.

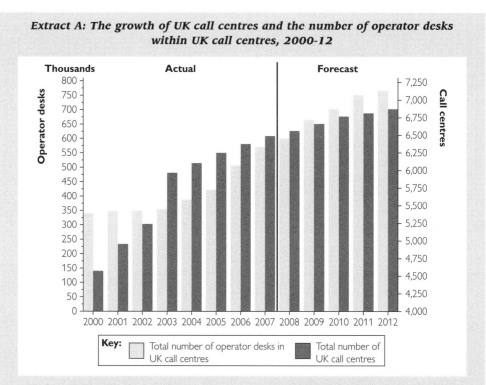

Extract A: The growth of UK call centres and the number of operator desks within UK call centres, 2000-12

Source: Official trade projections and forecasts

Note: Call centres contain operator desks from which the firm's employees (the operators) make telephone calls to clients or potential clients, or provide customer service advice to people phoning the call centre.

Extract B: The international mobility of the call centre industry

A call centre is a place of work in which call centre operators communicate by 1 telephone with a business's customers and potential customers. Call centres became one of the fastest growing sources of employment in the UK in the 1980s and 1990s. In recent years, call centres have moved abroad, often to the Indian subcontinent.

The rapid development of electronic methods of communication mean that service 5 providers such as call centres can now be located anywhere in the world, with little or no effect on the ability of call centres to provide services efficiently to their customers.

Four factors encouraging the overseas location of call centres are:
- relatively low wages in developing countries and eastern Europe
- highly reliable and cheap telecommunications 10
- 24-hour shift employment to overcome the problem of time zones
- workers fluent in the English language

Adapted from news sources

Extract C: Call centres and changes in service sector economic activity

The global market for call centre services is highly contestable and highly 1 competitive. To remain competitive, UK-based firms, such as the insurance company Activa, contract out (outsource) communicating with their customers to independent call centre companies located in developing countries.

In the 1980s and early 1990s, call centres became a major industry in Scotland and 5 the northeast of England, where wage rates are generally lower and unemployment higher than in southeast England. But in a global economy, there is no reason why call centres servicing British customers shouldn't be based in India. British companies are making dramatic savings by shifting the provision of back-office services, previously undertaken in-house, to India. 'Back-office' work includes 10 activities such as preparing business accounts, as well as providing customer service over the telephone.

Commentator Madan Mohan Rao sees this growth as the next global trend. 'This is a new form of economic shift' he says. 'First was the shift of low cost manufacturing from the west to China, Malaysia and so on. Now we're seeing the second wave. 15 Because of IT services and good telecommunications links, you can outsource a lot of the basic service and call centre jobs out of your country to other countries. UK call centres are going to find it increasingly difficult to compete.'

Adapted from news sources

Extract D: Should the government protect employment in UK call centres?

Speaking during a visit to a Bristol call centre, a government minister dismissed as a 1 'myth' the assertion that UK call centre sector was in 'terminal decline', despite a series of high profile financial services companies moving their call centre facilities overseas. 'The headlines announce thousands of jobs going to India and the far east, but the truth is that call centres in this country are still a thriving industry', she said. 5

3

data-response question

In response, the shadow industry secretary accused the government of 'complacency' over call centre jobs. He said that tens of thousands of workers have been sacked in the UK as firms have followed the exit sign out of the country. The movement of jobs in the long term will cripple UK competitiveness. 'For the trade secretary to encourage British companies to go for cheap labour over highly skilled, highly 10 motivated workers in Britain does not seem to be in the best interests of the British economy', he said.

Adapted from news sources

(1) Using Extract A, compare the number of call centres and the number of call centre operator desks located in the UK over the period shown by the data. (5 marks)

(2) Extract B mentions four factors that affect decisions to invest in new call centres in other countries. Analyse how two of these factors might influence the decision of a UK business to invest in a new call centre in the UK rather than overseas. (10 marks)

(3) Using the data and your economic knowledge, evaluate the view that the outsourcing abroad of service activities such as customer service and accounts inevitably improves the efficiency of British businesses. (25 marks)

■ ■ ■

Candidate's answer

(1) The numbers of call centres and call centre operator desks both increased over the period of actual measurement, 2000–07. The number of call centres increased from 4,000 to about 6,500 (63%), while the number of call centre operator desks increased from 330,000 to about 575,000 (74%). Both were also expected to increase over the rest of the data period, from 2008 to 2012, with call centre operator desks increasing at a faster rate than the number of call centres. **4/5 marks**

> *e* The candidate makes two points of comparison, but only the first point is backed up fully with evidence from the statistics. For this question, the mark scheme states that 3 marks can be given for a point of comparison backed up by evidence from the data, but only 1 mark if there is no data support. This means a total of 4 marks in this case. The statement that call centre operator desks were expected to increase at a faster rate from 2008 to 2012 does not provide sufficient evidence to earn the extra mark. Numbers should always be provided in answers to the first part of a data-response question.

(2) Two of the four listed factors are 'workers fluent in the English language' and 'highly reliable and cheap telecommunications'. For the first factor, service providers such as insurance companies have recorded a lot of dissatisfaction from their UK customers about the quality of service provided by overseas call centres. Sometimes the English spoken by call centre operators is difficult to understand, and the operators may be unfamiliar with British culture and idiom. If this is the case, UK companies may gain more in consumer satisfaction, and therefore, in their willingness to continue to buy their products or services, by paying the higher wages demanded by UK call centre operators. However, the fact that overseas call centre operators are often highly educated graduates, while UK operators are less well educated may counter this point.

If UK firms believed that communications are more likely to break down when communicating with overseas call centres, they might decide to locate their call centres in the UK instead. **4/10 marks**

🗒 This answer only earns 4 marks because it lacks appropriate analysis. The candidate could have explained how the factors might affect costs of production and thence profit. The statement about the reliability and low cost of electronic communication over thousands of miles could have been linked to firms' costs and profits. Investment decisions (synoptically relating to AS Unit 2) might also have been analysed. As it stands, the answer is too superficial.

(3) The two efficiency concepts particularly relevant for this question are productive efficiency and dynamic efficiency. For a firm, productive efficiency occurs when average costs of production are minimised. It is a static concept. By contrast, as the name indicates, dynamic efficiency refers to reductions in average costs occurring over time; for example, through a firm's growth, enabling it to benefit from economies of scale. The difference between (static) productive efficiency and dynamic efficiency is shown in the following diagram. If Firm A produces the level of output Q_1, it is productively efficient, but only in the static sense of a small firm that has not gained the benefits of economies of scale. Firm B is a much larger firm that has gained the benefits of economies of scale. Producing output Q_2, it is therefore dynamically efficient (as well as productively efficient), enjoying lower average costs than Firm A.

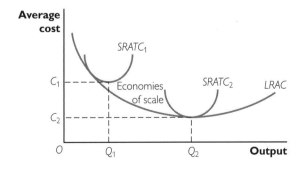

data-response question

However, dynamic efficiency extends beyond achieving lower average costs through gaining the benefits of economies of scale. It includes adopting more reliable methods of production which allow better quality goods to be produced, as well as innovation and research and development leading to the production of completely new types of good that did not previously exist.

Provided the four factors listed in Extract B enable a UK firm to reduce average costs of production, outsourcing abroad of service activities such as customer service and accounts should improve its productive efficiency. This can be illustrated by the firm's short-run average cost curve shifting downward, as shown below.

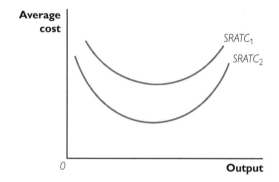

In the long run, outsourcing may also improve the firm's dynamic efficiency. However, when evaluating, the key word in the question is *inevitably*. It is more than likely, but not *inevitable*, that outsourcing abroad will improve productive and possibly dynamic efficiency. For the reason I explained in my answer to part (2), overseas location of call centres may lead to dissatisfaction among UK consumers. Location in a country such as the Congo, wracked by civil war, corruption and upheaval, is obviously likely to produce bad results than location in Bangalore, the city at the centre of the Indian telecommunications industry. And finally, even if outsourcing does improve a UK firm's efficiency, the effect may be extremely marginal. British Airways, for example, has outsourced much of its accounts division to India, but the benefits of this could possibly be adversely outweighed by bad management decisions in other areas of BA's operations, that could possibly bankrupt the company.   **21/25 marks**

📝 I have placed this answer just in Level 5. Several relevant issues have been identified and by starting the answer by homing in on productive and dynamic efficiency, the candidate shows a good understanding of economic concepts and principles. The evaluation is good rather than merely limited, leading to an overall Level 5 score.

Scored 30/40   75% = A* boundary

The European Union context

Question 4   The Single European Market and UK sports markets

Total for this question: 40 marks

Study **Extracts A**, **B**, and **C**, and then answer **all** parts of the question which follow.

Extract A: League positions and total annual wage bills of selected Premiership football clubs, May 2008

League position	Club	Wage bill
1	Manchester United	£121.1m
2	Chelsea	£172.0m
3	Arsenal	£101.3m
4	Liverpool	£90.0m
9	Manchester City	£54.2m
10	West Ham United	£44.2m
18	Reading	£33.0m
19	Birmingham	£26.6m
20	Derby County	£26.1m

Adapted from news sources

Extract B: Competitiveness and sports markets

Some professional sports — football, for example — provide an interesting mix of 1
competition and monopoly. In football, clubs compete in a league. The purpose of
competition is to win the league and to be generally successful from year to year.
In most conventional markets, becoming a monopoly by driving rivals out of business
represents ultimate success for a firm. But if a soccer club bankrupts all its rivals, 5
there is no one to play against. If Manchester United were to win the Premiership too
many times with too much ease, the league would become boring and fans would
lose interest. Scottish football, where Celtic and Rangers dominate, has already
suffered this problem, though the two leading teams are still well supported.

data-response question

Unlike most other businesses, in sport competitors need to collude to provide a 10
sellable product. The creation of a sporting spectacle requires teams to coordinate
times and venues for matches and to agree on the rules of competition. For most
businesses, competitors are a constraint on their commercial activities, but sports
teams have a peculiar interest in the viability of rivals. This collaborative element 15
requires careful treatment by anti-monopoly regulators.

Source: academic research paper

Extract C: Should footballers from other EU countries be allowed to work in the UK?

Before 1995, a professional footballer playing for a British football club could only 1
move to another club with the agreement of both clubs. Usually the agreement was
only reached by the setting of a 'transfer fee', through which the buying club
purchased the player from the selling club. The Union of European Football
Associations (UEFA) also administered a quota system which limited the number of 5
foreign players (from other EU states and from outside the EU) who could play in a
particular match.

In 1995, freedom of movement for labour within the Single European Market was
extended to footballers and other sports players. This made quota systems illegal. As
a result, English Premiership football clubs began to employ many more foreign 10
football players, especially those born in other EU member states. The number of
UK-born players employed by Premiership clubs fell. Some commentators argue that
this had an adverse effect on the quality and performance of England's national
football team. Not all agree. Some believe that because so few UK-born footballers
play in other EU leagues, the real problem lies in the poor quality of footballers that 15
UK countries produce. Foreign clubs do not want to hire English players because they
are not good enough.

In 2009, in response to pressure exercised by the UK government and by European
football authorities, Premiership clubs made a U-turn. They agreed to introduce a
quota system that requires eight of a squad of 25 players to be 'locally produced', with 20
at least four being trained at the club for at least 3 years between the ages of 16 and
21. Opponents of the rule change claim that an employment quota is an unjustifiable
restrictive practice which prevents the free movement of labour within the Single
European Market.

Adapted from news sources

(1) Using Extract A, identify two significant points of comparison between the league positions of Premiership football clubs at the end of the 2007/08 season and the total wages paid by each club during the season. (5 marks)

(2) 'The purpose of competition is to win...becoming a monopoly by driving rivals out of business represents ultimate success for a firm.' (Extract B, lines 2–5.) With the help of at least one diagram, analyse how competitive behaviour can lead to monopoly. (10 marks)

(3) '...an employment quota is an unjustifiable restrictive practice which prevents the free movement of labour within the Single European Market.' (Extract C, lines 22–24). Using the data and your economic knowledge, evaluate the view that sports markets within the UK have benefited from the complete freedom of labour within the Single European Market. (25 marks)

■ ■ ■

Candidate's answer

(1) A first point to note is that, with the exception of Chelsea, there is a negative correlation between the league position of clubs and the total amount spent on the wage bill. Thus Manchester United, which won the Premiership in first position, spent £121.1 million on wages, while Derby County, which ended up in the bottom twentieth position and were relegated, only spent £26.1 million on wages. As a second point, the greatest difference between the amount spent on wages between clubs which ended up next to each other in the final league table was £70.7 million, which separated Chelsea in second position and Arsenal in third position. **5/5 marks**

> 🄴 The question asks for two significant points of comparison. The candidate obeys this instruction and in each case provides sufficient evidence from the data to support each of the two comparative points. Full marks are therefore earned.

(2) In the context of the theory of the firm, economists generally assume that firms have a single business objective: to maximise profit. My diagram below illustrates the profit made by a pure monopoly, when there is only one firm in the market.

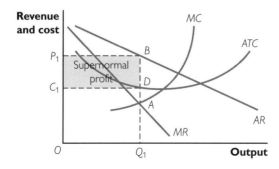

data-response question

The monopoly maximises profit, producing the level of output Q_1. The profit it makes divides into normal profit, which is treated as part of the monopoly's costs of production, and supernormal profit (monopoly profit) which is shown by the shaded rectangle. It can be shown that at any level of output above or below Q_1, the monopoly would make less profit. **6/10 marks**

When answering questions which relate to the theory of the firm, many candidates stray away from the thrust of the question by regurgitating notes they have learnt, in this case on a profit-maximising monopoly. This answer provides a good example of such drift. The answer earns only 1 mark out of the 6 available for written explanation. However, 5 marks are earned by the diagram. When a part (2) question explicitly asks for a diagram, around 5 marks are awarded for an accurate diagram. When the question does not ask for a diagram, marks can still be earned for a relevant diagram, but the total marks available would be less than 5. To earn more marks, the answer needs to develop the analysis of how, by driving rivals out of business, profit can be increased.

(3) A sports market is one in which professional sportsmen and women sell their labour in return for competing in a sport, or it may be a market in which teams compete against each other on a commercial basis, i.e. to earn money. The ability to earn money is usually directly related to the sporting success of the individual sportsman and/or the team that buys the sportsman's labour.

The Single European Market (SEM) has created free trade in goods within the European Union (EU). Goods can be traded between EU member states free of any import duties. The rules of the SEM also mean that there must be free movement of both capital and labour between member states.

It is the free movement of labour which is relevant to this question. As Extract C states, an employment quota, which restricts the number of workers from other EU states that can be employed in a particular EU country, is a restrictive practice, both a trading restrictive practice and a labour restrictive practice. Restrictive practices may benefit the people who impose the practice, but this may be at the expense of those whose freedom to compete is hampered.

Sports such as tennis, cricket, athletics and rugby have not really been affected by the SEM, or by employment quotas to restrict the free movement of sportsmen and women. The main sport that has been affected is football or soccer, which provides the scenario for the Extracts in this question. Free-market economic theory argues that free movement and trade in both goods and services, and in factors of production, increases economic welfare.

What is the evidence for this in the football market? On the plus side, unrestricted imports of foreign footballers have increased the quality of the product (entertaining football matches and the excitement of the Premier League). The Premiership has improved in quality, developing to become arguably better than competing overseas leagues in Spain, Italy and other EU countries. Match attendances have grown (at least until the onset of the 2008 recession), so more fans must be gaining more benefits. The players, both home-grown and from overseas, have also benefited, both from much higher wages and from the opportunities offered by free movement of labour.

On the debit side, many ordinary fans have lost out because they can no longer afford the high prices charged by the Premiership clubs for match tickets or for season tickets. Premiership games have become increasingly watched by so-called 'prawn sandwich fans', benefiting from corporate hospitality. But perhaps the main losers of all have been British-born football players. Extract C states that the number of UK-born players employed by Premiership clubs has fallen, and that this may have had an adverse effect on the quality and performance of England's national football team. However, the Extract also says that this may have had more to do with the lack of talent of UK-born players, maybe because they eat the wrong foods, binge drink and are badly trained. If this is the case, then complete freedom of labour within the Single European Market has definitely not completely benefited UK sports markets.

16/25 marks

e The candidate obviously knows a lot about sport, and about football in particular, so obeys the instruction to use both the data and his economic knowledge. He also discusses the cases for and against agreeing with the assertion that complete freedom of labour within the Single European Market has benefited UK sports markets. The answer starts well by explaining the meaning of restrictive practices in the context of the SEM. However, overall the answer lacks sufficient application of theory. The candidate mentions that free trade improves economic welfare, but this needs explaining. Synoptic application of trade theory learnt when studying Unit 4 would be relevant here. I have therefore placed the answer at the top of Level 3 (12–16 marks).

Scored 27/40   68% = grade A

ata-response question

Question 5   Overfishing and the EU's Common Fisheries Policy

Total for this question: 40 marks

Study **Extracts A**, **B and C**, and then answer **all** parts of the question which follow.

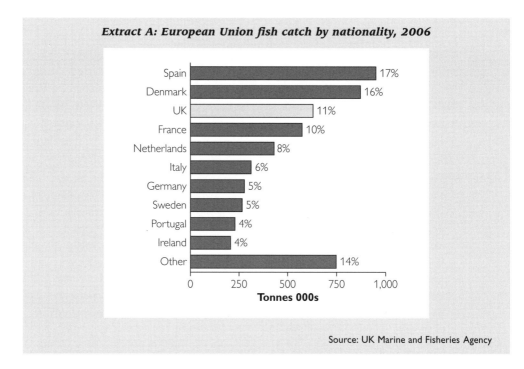

Extract A: European Union fish catch by nationality, 2006

Spain 17%
Denmark 16%
UK 11%
France 10%
Netherlands 8%
Italy 6%
Germany 5%
Sweden 5%
Portugal 4%
Ireland 4%
Other 14%

0   250   500   750   1,000
Tonnes 000s

Source: UK Marine and Fisheries Agency

Extract B: Are fish stocks public goods?

Unless the world's fish stocks are managed tightly by all concerned with fishing, they 1
may well collapse. People think they can take a limitless amount of the Earth's free
gifts, such as the atmosphere or the sea, or even, fish.

For centuries the Earth's fish stocks appeared to be free public goods. No prices were
attached to removing fish from the ocean, and so there was no need to impose 5
restraint on their use. For centuries, stocks of fish appeared to be non-excludable and
non-exhaustible. Property rights were not allocated to ownership of such an
abundant resource. Go ahead, fish to your heart's content, with ever more trawlers.
It's all free.

And for centuries, nothing harmful happens, such is the seemingly limitless 10
generosity of planet Earth. But on a finite globe, the limits logically have to be

reached at some stage. The North Sea separating Britain from mainland Europe is where most UK fishermen make their living. Decades of overfishing mean that British fishing boats are now fighting and competing with Spanish, Portuguese and French vessels for the dwindling bounty of the North Sea.   15

Source: Academic Research Paper

Extract C: The EU Common Fisheries Policy and the UK

Before the European Union's Common Fisheries Policy (CFP) was established in 1983, 1 the UK protected its own fishermen with a 12-mile fishing limit. This meant that Spanish, Portuguese and French fishing boats were prevented from fishing inside Britain's 12-mile limit. If caught doing so by fishery protection vessels, ship's captains could be heavily punished and equipment could be confiscated. Nevertheless, 5 because fishermen usually take the view that if they don't catch the fish, somebody else will, overfishing still occurred, both inside the fishing limit and out in the open seas beyond the area of local protection.

In 1983, the CFP opened up all the waters surrounding EU countries to every member EU state. At the same time, the EU tried to prevent the free-for-all, that seemed bound 10 then to occur, by imposing fishing quotas on the EU countries with fishing fleets. However, the Fisheries Policy did not work, leading to periodic reductions in fishing quotas, which then served to anger fishermen who were limited in the number of days in which they were legally allowed to fish. Needless to say, the policy was widely flouted.   15

The EU's executive, the European Commission, says more than 80% of Europe's fish stocks are now overfished. So EU member states are now being asked for their input on a new fisheries policy — one which officials promise will be radically different from the existing policy. A central aim is to minimise throwing discarded fish back into the sea. Discarding, usually of dead fish, occurs because fishermen have 20 exceeded their quotas or caught the wrong kind of fish.

The president of the UK's National Federation of Fishermen's Organisations, said: 'The CFP certainly needs to be scrapped because it's too vast, it covers such a huge range of waters...it's one cure fits all, only it doesn't work. We don't need faceless bureaucrats in Brussels who don't know a kipper from a cod telling us what we can 25 and can't catch.'

The environmental pressure group Greenpeace argues that Europe's fishing fleet needs to be halved in size. According to Greenpeace, the Common Fisheries Policy was created as a response to market failure, but it has led instead to significant government failure.   30

Adapted from news sources

data-response question

(1) Using Extract A, identify two significant points of comparison between the United Kingdom's total fish catch and that of other European Union countries in 2006. (5 marks)

(2) Extract B, lines 6–7, states that in the past, stocks of fish appeared to be non-excludable and non-exhaustible and that property rights were not allocated to ownership of such an abundant resource. Analyse this statement. (10 marks)

(3) '…the Common Fisheries Policy was created as a response to market failure, but it has led instead to significant government failure.' (Extract C, lines 28–30.) In the light of this statement, evaluate the view that abandoning the Common Fisheries Policy would inevitably benefit the UK economy. (25 marks)

■ ■ ■

Candidate's answer

(1) Producing around 600 000 tonnes of fish and 11% of the EU total, the UK was in third position in terms of total catch, behind Spain (around 900 000 tonnes and 17%) and Denmark (around 850 000 tonnes and 16%). The UK, with a population of about 60 million, caught 65% more of the EU's total fish catch than Germany, the country with the largest population in the EU, though this was probably due to the fact that Germany has a much shorter coastline. **5/5 marks**

> The candidate makes two significant points of comparison, backed up in each case by evidence from the data, so earns all 5 marks. The answer drifts into offering a correct but irrelevant explanation for the second point of comparison, but this is not serious as little time is wasted. But to reinforce the point I made for Question 1, part (1) questions require comparison (and sometimes identification), but not explanation.

(2) Most goods are private goods which are excludable. The owner of private goods such as fruit in a greengrocery, can stop people gaining the benefits of apples and pears in the shop, unless customers pay for the goods. (Obviously this is not the case when people successfully shop lift.) Shopkeepers possess property rights over the goods they have bought and which they wish to sell. Selling the goods transfers the property rights to the new owners.

By contrast, outside of national fishing limits, nobody owns the fish swimming in the ocean, so nobody possesses and can exercise property rights over fish stocks. Without international law being changed, and then enforced and policed, it is impossible to prevent fishing boats catching fish for free. The oceans' fish are therefore largely non-excludable. But though non-excludable, ocean fish are certainly nowadays exhaustible. Overfishing depletes the fish stock, perhaps eventually below a critical level beyond which the fish stock cannot replace itself. However, this was not true in the past when fishing technology was primitive and there was a super-abundance of ocean fish. **10/10 marks**

(3) The market failure that the Common Fisheries Policy was created to correct, was the one I described in my previous answer — namely the problem of overfishing resulting from the public good nature of fish stocks, particularly those in the North Sea which separates the UK from continental Europe.

However, the CFP has failed to solve this problem, and by abolishing nationally imposed and policed fishing limits, arguably the policy has made the problem worse. The problem is an example of what is called the 'tragedy of the commons'. The tragedy describes a situation in which herdsmen add to the number of cattle each of them grazes on a commons until overgrazing results in an outcome from which all the herdsmen suffer. In this case, the North Sea is the commons, and the owners of fishing boats overfish waters that are open to all. The CFP tries to prevent overfishing by imposing quotas. This has not worked, partly because of the problem of enforcing the quotas. The owner of a fishing boat takes the view that if he keeps to the quota, other boats will not, so in the short term he, but not they, will suffer. If all, or most, owners adopt this view, quotas are not kept, overfishing and fish stock depletion occur, and the market failure gets worse. The CFP's attempt to correct the market failure has failed and arguably made the problem worse, so government failure occurs.

12/25 marks

This answer is good as far as it goes but it does not go far enough. The candidate explains and analyses the statement that heads the question, but does not go on to address the question itself, namely whether abandoning the Common Fisheries Policy will inevitably benefit the UK economy. A relevant argument would be the significance of the fisheries industry for the British economy. Britons do not eat much fish compared to the inhabitants of France, Spain and Portugal, but the money earned from exporting fish is important for the balance of payments. The fishing industry is also an important part of regional economies, for example, in eastern Scotland. A good answer should also consider what might happen if the CFP is abandoned. Would it be even more of a free-for-all in the North Sea, or would the UK be able to exercise greater control in the UK national interest by effectively policing territorial waters that extend far beyond the UK coastline?

Finally, many (3) data-response questions and part (2) essay questions include words such as *must*, *always*, *solely*, and in this question *inevitably*. Key words such as these must be addressed in order to show good evaluative skills. So, in spite of the good analysis, because the question has not been properly answered, I have placed this answer at the bottom of Level 3 (12–16 marks, an adequate answer with some correct analysis but very limited evaluation).

Scored 27/40   68% = low-grade A

d 6 ata-response question

Question 6 EU labour migration and the UK

Total for this question: 40 marks

Study **Extracts A**, **B** and **C**, and then answer **all** parts of the question which follow.

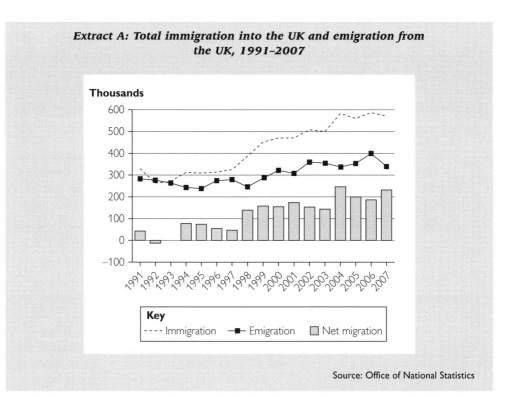

Extract A: Total immigration into the UK and emigration from the UK, 1991–2007

Source: Office of National Statistics

Extract B: Is net migration from Poland into Britain coming to an end?

At the beginning of 2007, Kris Ploski employed 50 Polish builders working in his 1
construction firm. By the end of 2007, that had suddenly changed. 'It hit me hard',
said Ploski, 'Nearly 30% of my team didn't come back after Christmas'. From
agriculture to construction you will find a similar story.

So why were Poles forsaking high wages, guaranteed employment and bad weather 5
for a less certain future back home? One expert says the decision is mostly down to
simple economics and how this affects those Polish migrants (most of them) who
send a proportion of their earnings home. Official statistics showed that a
combination of recession and a plummeting pound — which reduced the value of

remittances home — led to a record emigration from the UK of Poles and other 10 workers from the new EU member states in central Europe.

In 2007, a spokesman for the Institute for Public Policy Research had asked: 'What will happen to the UK economy if these large numbers of Poles stop coming?' In sectors such as farming and food processing, he warned, there are serious questions about how they will remain sustainable if the labour supply dries up. The farm sector 15 would be in dire straits without the immigrants willing to do the hard graft on the land. But in agriculture, the typical worker's overtime pay fell sharply at the time that migrants began to work on farms. In hotels and restaurants, basic pay fell too. One local man coming out of the dole office said: 'I'd prefer to sign on than do the jobs that migrant workers do'. 20

Is a Polish exodus good news for British workers? Some business leaders believe the Poles have allowed us to paper over fundamental problems within our economy. The chief executive of the British Chambers of Commerce, said 'There is an attitude and work ethic problem in certain parts of the UK, where people do not see the need or have the desire to work'. 25

Adapted from news sources

Extract C: Who profited from the Polish plumbers?

Over 600 000 Poles came to work in the UK after Poland joined the European Union 1 in May 2004. Scores of UK businesses then thrived from the £4bn of income earned by Polish plumbers, builders, bar staff, waiters, nannies and other migrant workers. In response, some of the biggest names in British business began to 'go Polish'. In 2007, the supermarket group J Sainsbury started selling 32 Polish foods. 5

'At least, they are waking up', said the business development manager of *Polish Express*, one of the eight newspapers printed in the UK that came into existence to target migrants from Poland. 'To start with, British businesses just did not realise the opportunities'. But now Barclays Bank is bending over backwards to attract customers from the growing Polish migrant community, which has become just as 10 important as that for any other ethnic community.

However, migration from countries such as Poland imposes costs upon the UK economy, which may have to be paid for through higher tax rates. A small number of schools saw a significant increase in admissions. Some local authorities reported problems of overcrowding in private housing. There have been cost pressures on 15 English language training.

So what impact has the Polish consumer had on British businesses? 'It was basically like adding the consumer demand of Liverpool to the economy in just 2 years', said the Chief Executive of the Centre for Economics and Business Research, a think tank.

Adapted from news sources

data-response question

(1) Using Extract A, identify two significant features of the migration between
the **UK** and the rest of the world over the period shown by the data. **(5 marks)**

(2) '....in agriculture, the typical worker's overtime pay fell sharply at the
time that migrants began to work on farms. In hotels and restaurants,
basic pay fell too.' (Extract B, lines 17–18.)

With the use of a labour market diagram, analyse how migration from
eastern Europe has affected both wage rates and employment in **UK**
agricultural, hotel or restaurant industries. **(10 marks)**

(3) Do you agree that the benefits for the **UK** economy of migration from
other EU countries have exceeded the costs? Justify your answer. **(25 marks)**

■ ■ ■

Candidate's answer

(1) The first significant feature is that there was net migration into the UK for every
single year in the data series except 1992 and 1993. Net migration into the UK
rose from about 50 000 in 1991, the first year in the series, to a peak of about
230 000 in 2004. The number was only slightly smaller in 2007, the last year in
the series. The data shows thousands of foreign scroungers coming into Great
Britain and taking our jobs. The second significant feature is immigration per
year rose over the whole 16-year period, but emigration fell. Immigration rose
from about 330 000 in 1991 to about 580 000 in 2007, an increase of about 75%
comparing the first and last year in the series. Emigration fell from about
290 000 to about 240 000, or about 17%, again comparing the first and last year.
5/5 marks

> ✏ Although the candidate gives an early indication of the rant he is later to indulge
> in when answering the last part of the question, he does all that is required to
> earn full marks for this part of the question. Note the wording of the question,
> which asks for two significant features of Extract A to be identified, and not for
> a comparison of two data series. Similar wording is most likely when Extract A
> contains just a single data series. In this question, there are two (indeed three)
> data series, but the question does not ask for a comparison.

(2) Immigration from eastern Europe has shifted the supply curve of labour to the
right in the labour market for farm workers. Before immigration, the farm wage
rate was W_1. The shift to the right of the supply curve as immigrants flood the
market leads to an excess supply of labour. More farm workers wish to work at
wage rate W_1 than farmers wish to hire. The excess supply of labour causes the
equilibrium wage rate to fall to a level that clears the market, namely W_2. Total
employment has increased (from L_1 to L_2), but this masks the fact that
immigrants rather than British farm workers have the new jobs. There has been
an increase in supply and an extension of demand. **9/10 marks**

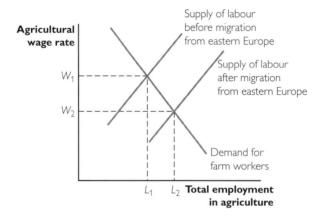

Agricultural wage rate

Supply of labour before migration from eastern Europe

Supply of labour after migration from eastern Europe

W_1

W_2

Demand for farm workers

L_1 L_2 **Total employment in agriculture**

ℯ Despite a second hint of xenophobia, this is a good answer, which earns 5 marks for the diagram and 4 marks for the written explanation. With this type of question, it is important to remember the advice given when answering similar questions at AS, namely to *analyse* (at A2) rather than *describe* in the written part of the answer. The candidate analyses why the wage rate falls in response to excess supply appearing in the labour market. To earn full marks, the candidate would have to offer a second reason for the wage rate falling, e.g. the absence of a trade union with power to prevent the fall, or wage differences between the UK and eastern Europe attracting migrants into the UK labour market.

(3) Migration of labour from other European Union countries takes jobs away from British workers. All governments have a duty to look after the interests of their own people, and this means protecting their jobs. Far stricter immigration controls should be imposed, and if it is necessary to do this, Britain should leave the European Union. It is a completely inefficient bureaucracy, ruling us from Brussels, and staffed by hundreds of thousands of eurocrats who we pay for. British taxes should be used to subsidise British workers, and not to pay the inflated salaries of unproductive foreign civil servants who want to do down the British economy. There are only a certain amount of jobs available, and we should have them and not Germans and Italians who we beat in the Second World War.

The only case for allowing Polish workers into the UK is at least they are Europeans and not immigrants from Africa, who have little to offer to the UK economy and usually end up in prison. There are only benefits to be gained from preventing foreign workers coming over here and stealing our jobs. There are no costs involved. As Extract B states, immigrant workers drive down wages, thereby harming hard-working decent British workers.   **3/25 marks**

ℯ This answer is a classic rant that shows little evidence that the candidate has actually studied economics. The answers to the earlier parts of the question

data-response question

show that the candidate does understand economic theory, but he has now evidently got rather carried away. Questions on labour migration, together with questions on the European Union, tend to produce a disproportionate number of rants. As this question covers both these emotive topics, the tendency to rant has been magnified. This candidate has certainly worked up a head of steam. Whatever your political views, you need to keep them out of your answers. Engaging in a rant will do you no good in an economics exam. Pretend you are a neutral consultant being paid to give impartial advice to your clients.

The answer is restricted to Level 1. The descriptor for Level 1 (0–6 marks) is: 'A very weak answer: few, if any, relevant issues are recognised. Economic concepts and principles are not adequately understood or applied to the question. No satisfactory analysis or evaluation, the answer generally fails to answer the question. There is little use of economic terminology'. However, 3 marks were earned in this case because the candidate mentioned that inward migration might drive down UK wages. There is little else of any worth. It is theoretically unsound to argue the 'lump of labour' theory, which assumes there is always a fixed amount of jobs, and that workers from overseas inevitably take jobs from British workers. But, despite the poor quality of this answer, the answers to the first two parts of the question enabled the candidate to scrape a grade D for the question taken as a whole.

Scored 17/40   43% = low-grade D

Essay questions

Question 1   Perfect competition, monopoly and the water industry

(1) Explain how the equilibrium price and level of output are achieved in a perfectly competitive market, both for the whole market and for one firm within the market. **(15 marks)**

(2) In the UK, firms in the water industry, such as Thames Water, are regional monopolies. Evaluate different policies the government could use to deal with the problems posed by monopoly in the water industry. **(25 marks)**

Candidate's answer

(1) Perfect competition is defined by six conditions. These are: a very large number of buyers and sellers; each of whom have perfect market information; each of whom can buy or sell as much as they wish at the ruling market price; each of whom is unable by their own actions to influence the market price; a homogeneous, uniform or identical product; and last, complete freedom of market entry and exit in the long run, but not in the short run.

The diagram I have drawn below shows a perfectly competitive firm maximising profit. Profit is the difference between total revenue (TR) and total cost (TC). At low levels of output, the firm would make a loss because to start with, total costs are greater than total sales revenue. This is because the firm still has to pay fixed costs even when output and sales are zero and no revenue is being earned. The firm breaks even (i.e. makes zero profit or loss) at the level of output at which the TR curve crosses the TC curve. Profits are made at levels of output above this point. Maximum profits are made at Q_1 where the TR and TC curves are furthest apart. Profits are shown by the vertical distance AB, and by the difference between R_1 and C_1 on the vertical axis.

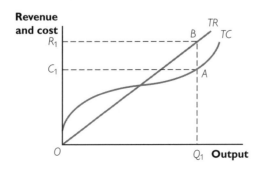

essay question

However, the diagram above shows a perfectly competitive firm in short-run equilibrium, making supernatural profit. My second diagram (below) shows long-run equilibrium. In the long run, the *TR* curve lies above the *TC* curve at all points *but one* on the *TC* curve. This is the point *X*, at which the perfectly-competitive firm makes natural profit only at output *Q**. At this level of output *TR* = *TC*. When producing *Q**, there is no incentive for firms to enter or leave the market, hence long-run equilibrium. (Equilibrium means a state of balance or rest.)

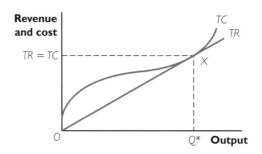

9/15 marks

📝 There are two ways of using a diagram to show the equilibrium profit-maximising firm in perfect competition (and indeed in monopoly). The way you have probably been taught (and which is in the Content Guidance section of this book) uses average and marginal cost and revenue curves and the profit-maximising rule: *MR* = *MC*. The alternative way, which this candidate adopts, is to use total revenue and total cost curves. Unfortunately this analysis is generally more limited. For example, neither of the diagrams in the answer shows the ruling market price, which is the price the profit-maximising perfectly competitive firm passively accepts. The diagrams do show the firm's level of output (Q_1 and *Q**) in the short run and the long run, but not the market level of output for the market as a whole (which comprises all the firms in the market).

Candidates often approach exam questions on perfect competition by churning out the six conditions of perfect competition and leaving the answer at that. This candidate starts off with the conditions of perfect competition, but fortunately then develops the answer. Note the common error in the answer, namely the mention of 'supernatural' profit instead of 'supernormal' profit (and 'natural' profit instead of 'normal' profit). The examiner would probably treat this as a slip and not penalise the candidate, unless the answer was riddled with further errors and nonsense. For this answer, I have awarded 2 marks for the conditions of perfect competition (definitional marks), 4 marks for the diagrams, and 3 marks for explaining the perfectly competitive firm's level of output in the short run and the long run.

(2) The policies I am going to analyse and evaluate to deal with the problems of monopoly posed by water companies such as Thames Water are breaking up the monopolies (monopoly 'busting') and regulating the monopolies. I shall analyse breaking up the water monopolies with the aid of the following diagram:

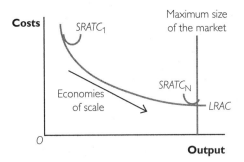

Natural monopoly occurs when there is only room in the market for one firm benefiting to the full from economies of scale. Because of the nature of its product, the water industry — which is a utility industry — experiences a particular marketing problem. The industry delivers water through a distribution network of pipes into millions of separate businesses and homes. Competition in the provision of distribution networks is extremely wasteful, since it requires the duplication of fixed capacity, therefore causing each supplier to incur unnecessarily high fixed costs. Hence the case for monopoly. Natural monopolies are difficult to split into competitive smaller companies without a significant loss of economies of scale and productive efficiency. If a large number of water companies competed for business, each would incur much higher average costs of production, depicted on the short-run average cost curve $SRATC_1$ on my diagram. By contrast, the monopoly benefits from the lower average costs associated with $SRATC_N$, because economies of scale have been benefited from to the full. According to this line of reasoning, breaking up a natural monopoly is like 'throwing out the baby with the bathwater', i.e. competition is achieved but at the expense of abandoning economies of scale.

However, there is always a danger that a monopoly, if allowed to continue to exist, will exploit its consumers by hiking up prices to cover unnecessary costs. It may be content with an easy life, but riddled with X-inefficiency. This is where regulation comes in. If an external regulator is appointed who imposes a price cap rule and who possesses the ability to fine the monopoly for monopoly abuse, the monopoly can be made to behave itself. But the regulator may be too weak, he may side with the regulated company rather than with consumers (regulatory capture) and he possesses insufficient technical knowledge to regulate effectively.

However, provided the regulator can do his job properly, I believe that the two policies of allowing a monopoly to persist in the water industry (rather than

essay question

breaking it up) and external regulation can work effectively. This is because, for the reasons I have explained, monopoly busting will not be effective, due to the natural monopoly position of water companies. Other policies could also be used, either in tandem or in place of regulation. These include imposing a windfall profit tax on water companies, and taking the water companies back into state ownership, in which case they will again become nationalised industries.   **23/25 marks**

This is an excellent answer that reaches Level 5 (good analysis and good evaluation). I have resisted the temptation to award full marks, because only two policy options are analysed and evaluated, though two more are mentioned as a bit of an afterthought in the last sentence of the answer. A raw mark of 80% is achieved for the answers to the two parts of the essay. However, this would probably translate into a UMS mark of 90% or more, hence the A* grade for the question considered as a whole.

Scored 32/40   80% = grade A*

ssay question

Question 2 Price-setting for a rock concert

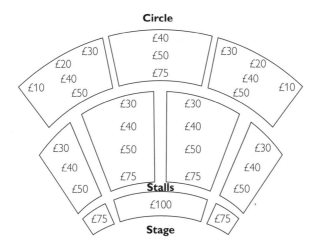

Circle

The prices above are charged by an arena for tickets to see a rock concert

(1) **Explain why different prices are charged for tickets for events such as rock concerts.** (15 marks)

(2) **Evaluate the economic reasons for and against charging the same price for every ticket at such events.** (25 marks)

Candidate's answer

(1) The theory of price discrimination explains why different prices are charged for different tickets at events such as rock concerts. According to the question, prices ranging from a high of £100 to a low of £10 are charged by the arena for tickets to see the rock concert. However, to explain why different prices are charged, I shall pretend that there are only two different prices: £75 and £50. I shall also assume that 'diehard' fans of the rock group playing at the concert are prepared to pay £75, whereas 'ordinary' fans are only prepared to pay £50. This means that the two different groups of fans have different price elasticities of demand and different demand curves, which are shown on my diagram below.

essay question

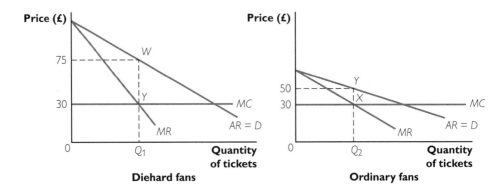

Diehard fans **Ordinary fans**

At all the prices that could be charged for seeing the rock concert, diehard demand is more inelastic than ordinary demand — indicating that the latter fans are less enthusiastic about the group performing at the rock concert. For both groups of fans, the downward-sloping demand curves in my diagram show average revenue (AR), but not marginal revenue (MR). In each case, the MR curve is twice as steep as the AR curve. The diagrams also assume (unrealistically) that the marginal cost (MC) of selling an extra ticket is always the same, namely £30. This explains the horizontal MC curve in both panels of the diagram.

To maximise profit, MR must equal MC in both sub-markets. As the diagrams show, this means that diehard fans pay the higher price of £75 for admission, with ordinary fans paying the lower entry price of £50. With the different prices being charged, Q_1 diehard fans and Q_2 ordinary fans watch the concert. The different prices charged result from the different price elasticities of demand. Profit is maximised when more price-sensitive ordinary fans pay less than the less price-sensitive diehard fans. **10/15 marks**

e The question does not mention price discrimination. However, the candidate addresses the question with a thorough and focused explanation of how price discrimination leads to different prices being charged. The answer earns all the 10 marks available in the mark scheme for a single line of explanation. In this case, the question does not ask for a diagram, but the mark scheme allows 3 marks for a relevant and accurate diagram, which is provided in this answer. Nevertheless, when a diagram is not mentioned in the question, full marks can be earned without a diagram. However, full marks also require more than one possible explanation. The candidate could have argued that the seats in an arena or concert hall are not homogeneous. For example, a seat in the front row of the stalls is a better 'product' with a better view of the stage than a seat at the end of the back row in the circle. Firms usually charge higher prices for better quality products. Also, prices might vary according to the fame of the rock artists delivering the concert. Ticket prices for a Coldplay concert are likely to be higher than for a little-known singer or band.

(2) The main reason in favour of charging the same price for tickets is that identical prices increase consumer surplus compared to the situation when there is price discrimination. Consumer surplus is the economic welfare enjoyed by consumers. I shall use the diagram below, which is a more sophisticated version of my earlier diagram, to explain why.

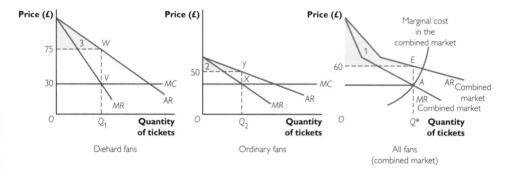

If different prices are charged to diehard and ordinary fans in my earlier example, firms increase profit by taking consumer surplus away from consumers and converting it into extra monopoly profit or supernormal profit. The left-hand and centre panels of the diagram are the same as the two panels in my earlier diagram, but I have added an extra panel to show the combined market (diehard and ordinary fans). The combined market shows the average revenue curves added together, and likewise the marginal revenue curves.

If all fans pay the same price (£60), the consumer surplus they enjoy is shown by the shaded area (numbered 1) lying above £60 in the right-hand panel of the diagram. But if diehard fans are charged £75 a ticket while ordinary fans pay only £50, surplus falls to equal the shaded areas numbered 3 and 2 in the left-hand and centre panels. (The shaded areas 3 and 2 are smaller in size than shaded area 1.) With price discrimination, the arena owner's profit has increased by transferring consumer surplus from consumers to the producer. Producer welfare (producer surplus) has increased at the expense of consumer welfare (consumer surplus). To prevent this happening, all the rock fans at the concert should be charged the same price.

The main reason against charging the same price to all consumers is that it is not fair for the arena owner who takes the entrepreneurial risk in putting on the concert. However, I think that this is a much weaker argument than that used to justify identical prices, so in conclusion, I believe that different prices should not be charged. Also, this is much fairer for consumers. **16/25 marks**

✍ To emphasise once again, when answering the second part of an essay question (or the third part of a data-response question), to earn a high mark you have to evaluate as well as analyse. This answer is strong on analysis but the evaluation

essay question

is limited. The descriptor for Level 3 is 'An adequate answer with some analysis but limited evaluation'. In this answer, the analysis is good, though in a strictly narrow sense because it does not extend beyond analysing the effect of identical prices and price discrimination on consumer surplus. Overall, the answer reaches high Level 3 (16 marks out of the available 25 marks), but gets no higher. Level 4 requires several, rather than a few, issues being recognised. This answer does not meet this descriptor. Most of the answer focuses on a single benefit of charging the same price to all customers. The case against is extremely cursory and a bit of an add-on. This means there is little scope for evaluation. When evaluating, be warned about using the words *fair* and *unfair*. Both these words are normative, and what is fair for you may not be fair for me. If you use these words, you must use evidence to justify your judgement.

Scored 26/40   65% = A/B boundary

Question 3 The causes of poverty and government policies to reduce poverty

(1) Explain the causes of poverty in the United Kingdom today. (15 marks)

(2) Evaluate the view that poverty can best be reduced through the use of progressive taxation and transfers in the government's fiscal policy. (25 marks)

Candidate's answer

(1) Before explaining the *causes* of poverty, it is first necessary to define poverty itself. Economists define two types of poverty, *absolute* poverty and *relative* poverty, though other forms of poverty such as *fuel* poverty (people are fuel poor if they are spending at least 10% of their income on energy) are also identified.

According to the *Poverty Site*, absolute poverty refers to a set standard which is the same in all countries and which does not change over time, for example living on an income of less than $2 a day. In India, absolute poverty is defined as the inability to afford 800 calories a day. By this criterion, hardly anyone in the UK is in poverty. By contrast, relative poverty refers to a standard which is defined in terms of the society in which an individual lives and which, therefore, differs between countries and over time. In the UK, a household is regarded as relatively poor if household income is less than 60% of median household income. *Social exclusion* is a particularly relevant poverty concept. Social exclusion relates to alienation or disenfranchisement of certain people within society.

The graph below shows the measurement of relative poverty in the UK in 2007/08. £393 was the median household income, which meant that all households with an income on or below £235 a week were deemed to be relatively poor.

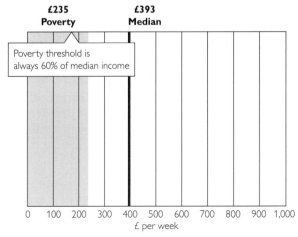

£235
Poverty

£393
Median

Poverty threshold is always 60% of median income

0   100   200   300   400   500   600   700   800   900   1,000
£ per week

essay question

Virtually all the people who are relatively poor in the UK are not absolutely poor. In this essay, I am going to explain the causes of relative poverty in the UK today. Two of the main causes are old age and unemployment. Poverty caused by old age primarily affects old people who rely on the state pension and lack a private pension. Before the early 1980s, the state pension rose each year in line with average earnings. This meant that pensioners shared in the increase in national prosperity delivered by economic growth and higher real earnings. However, in recent decades, the state pension has risen in line with the retail prices index (RPI) rather than with average earnings. As a result, the real value of the state pension has stayed at the level it reached a generation ago, though the real earnings of those in work have continued to rise. Unemployment benefits are also now linked to the RPI and, for similar reasons as the state pension, have fallen behind average earnings. **10/15 marks**

It is always best to start your answer to the first part of an essay question by defining terms or concepts which are in the question or which are relevant to the question (just as you should for a part (2) answer to a data-response question). The mark scheme allows a few marks to be earned through providing appropriate definitions. However, in this case, the candidate goes over the top and wastes too much valuable exam time by elaborating the definitions. Two short, sharp statements are all that is required to pick up the available marks for definitions. The candidate would have been better off writing more about the *causes* of poverty (relative or absolute). *Causes* is in the plural, so at least two causes must be explained. The candidate deals with old age well, but the explanation of how unemployment causes relative poverty needs more development. The answer could explain how, in the recession which started in 2008, the number of people unemployed grew to reach nearly 3 million in 2009, thus increasing the number of households suffering relative poverty. Also, to increase the chance of earning full marks, it is always a good idea to explain, in this case, a third cause of relative poverty, for example low wages. I have awarded 2 marks for definitions, 6 marks for the first explanation offered, and 2 marks for the second explanation.

(2) Progressive taxation occurs when the proportion of total income paid in tax increases as income increases. Transfers are benefit payments, for example the state pension and unemployment pay, paid for out of tax revenues, and given by the government to claimants. Both are a part of the government's fiscal policy. Fiscal policy is the part of the government's overall economic policy in which it uses taxation, public spending and its budgetary position (deficit, surplus or balanced budget) to achieve its chosen policy objectives.

The diagram below illustrates how progressive taxation and transfers can reduce relative poverty. If relative poverty is measured in terms of disposable income, which is income after the receipt of transfers and payment of income tax, it is obvious that transfers and progressive taxation reduce relative poverty by squeezing the incomes of the rich and boosting the incomes of the poor.

Therefore it is true that relative poverty can be reduced by the two fiscal policy measures. However, absolute poverty, in so far as it exists in the UK, may not be reduced. This is because the absolutely poor are the destitute and homeless, often living on the street. Often, they fail to claim benefits because they are not registered to do so, and they are too poor to pay income tax.

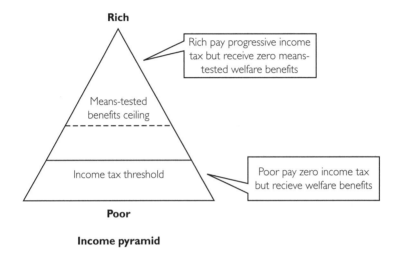

Income pyramid

11/25 marks

In contrast to part (1) of an essay answer, the levels mark scheme for part (2) does not explicitly provide marks for definitions. Nevertheless, it is always appropriate to provide definitions since they provide a platform on which to develop the answer.

Overall, however, this answer is unbalanced and ultimately disappoints. The candidate explains how progressive taxation and transfers can reduce poverty. The explanation is particularly good for relative poverty, but is less good for absolute poverty. In this case, the fact that the absolutely poor are too poor to pay income tax is neither here nor there. The way to reduce absolute poverty is to give transfer payments to the poorest people in society, and, even better, to give them jobs. The candidate might also have argued that a poverty trap (or earnings trap) might emerge if the two policies of progressive taxation and means-tested benefits are used together. This could lead into discussion of disincentive effects and how these might affect economic growth.

The real problem with this answer is that it does not discuss whether poverty can *best* be reduced through the use of progressive taxation and transfers. This wording should send the signal to candidates that alternatives to progressive taxation and transfers should be introduced and briefly analysed, before being evaluated along with the two policy measures in the question. Alternative

essay question

measures could be: promoting economic growth and creating more jobs, raising the national minimum wage, raising the retirement age and making the sacking of elderly workers illegal, and using tax credits. The latter links in with progressive taxation and transfers, but is a slightly different element of fiscal policy. However, the candidate has done none of this, and thus has not properly answered the question. For this reason I have awarded a high Level 2 mark, since the answer displays no evaluation and its analysis is too narrow.

Scored 21/40   53% = mid-grade C